A TEXAN'S ADVENTURE IN SWITZERLAND

A Texan's Adventure in SWITZERLAND

RANDY SNOW

Snowdog91 Productions
Mesa, Az
2023

Library of Congress Control Number: 2023908580

ISBN: 979-8-9871618-0-7

Edited by: Antonia Murphy www.antoniamurphy.com
Cover Design: Tayyab
Formatting: Natalya Belova
Map sketch: Teo Aladashvili

This book is dedicated to my family, those related by blood and those related by a special bond.
Thank you for loving me and always being there for me.

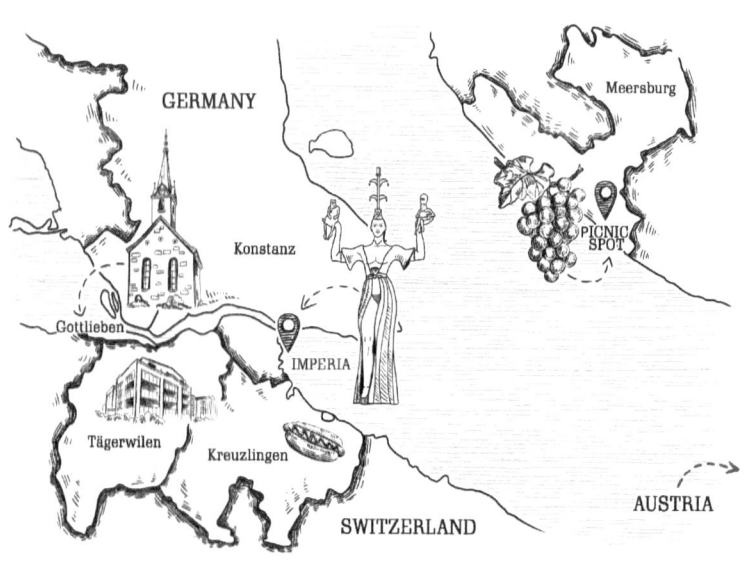

GERMANY

Meersburg

Konstanz

Gottlieben

IMPERIA

PICNIC
SPOT

Tägerwilen

Kreuzlingen

SWITZERLAND

AUSTRIA

CONTENTS

Prologue: The End 1

The Crash 3

Headed To Switzerland 7

Cowboy 11

Alarm Bells 17

Crack Drugs 21

Filet Mignon 27

No Sacks 31

Secret Society 37

First Days 43

Papers Please 47

Bang, Bang 51

Money Launderer 55

Rheinschwimmen 59

Cowboy 65

Test Time 71

Black Forest 75

Bodensee Blues 83

Newbie 93

Into The Void 103

Eva 109

Dove Fare Pipì 113

Goat Dog 121

007...125
Fáe! Fáe!...129
Aggies...131
The Day Cowboy Got Old 137
Birthday...139
Last Hike..143
Thump 147
A Letter From Luna...............................151
Baby Girl..155
Making it Official................................157
2020..161
Four-Handed Belly Rub...........................167
Hitched..171
Last Day...175
Angel..179
Epilogue: The Beginning 181

Acknowledgments.................................185

PROLOGUE: THE END

The day after I launched over the handlebars of my motorcycle and smashed into the pavement, my phone rang.

I was propped up on the couch with a cup of coffee, wincing from the pain of the raw wounds up and down my left side. I glanced at my phone.

Work was calling. *That's nice,* I thought. *They must be checking up on me. Maybe they want to send me an edible bouquet.* I picked up the call.

"Randy?" rasped an unfamiliar voice. "This is Janine from HR. I'm sorry to inform you that your services are no longer required at NEC America. In keeping with company policy, you will receive four weeks' severance, and your medical insurance will be canceled after 90 days. Do you have any questions?"

"Um. No edible bouquet?" I stammered. But Janine didn't laugh.

My body was broken, and now I was unemployed. And that was the end of my life as I knew it.

THE CRASH

I'm on my way home from having dinner with some friends.
It's always good to sit down over a meal and catch up, find
out how the families are doing, what's going on at work.
After dinner we say our goodbyes and I head out to my
bike. It's a fall evening, and even in Texas it's a little chilly.
I zip up my jacket to stay warm and put my helmet on. My
custom Harley Sportster 1200 starts with a roar and a purr,
and I can hear the crunch of the fallen leaves under my
tires. It's not fancy, but it's a nice bike—blue, black, and
chrome, with long front pegs. Small enough to get around
town easily, but big enough to go out on the road.

Picking up speed, the wind blows across my face, crisp
and refreshing. It's peaceful on my bike, and soon my mind
wanders. *Just one more day of the grind and then I have a whole
week off for Thanksgiving.* My folks are coming to see me
and I'm thinking about all the last-minute things I need
to do before they get here. *Pick up some real food, especially
some fruits and veggies so they think I'm eating healthy. Make
the guest bed. Clean up—*

That was a mistake.

The thing about riding a motorcycle is, you're a lot
smaller than the other cars on the road. As I approach an

intersection, the large delivery van on my right puts on his turn signal and slows down to make a right turn. I zoom past him, trying to remember what else I need to do. Then I glance to my right. *Oh God, a dark Honda Civic and it's on a collision course with my legs.*

There's no time to react. I crank as hard as I can on the throttle. My bike lurches forward just enough to save my legs, but not me. As the Honda slams into my bike, I hear a loud booming sound as metal smashes into metal and all I can think of is the Batman comic book with me, my bike being hit by a car, and a large BAM! written next to it. As the force of the impact spins my bike around, I'm catapulted into the air. In the next frame of the comic book, I'm flung through the air with a caption: *Look Mom, I'm flying.*

After the initial blow of my body smacking into concrete, I go into a roll to minimize the damage and eventually end up in a slide. I'm skidding down the road, my motorcycle up ahead of me. Sparks are flying everywhere. Time slows down. The sparks look like embers from a bonfire, rising and floating up into the night. Then I realize: I'm not wearing protection on my legs, just an old pair of Levi's, and as the denim tears away I can feel the road grinding away at my flesh. Trying to limit the damage to my lower body, I lean into my shoes and riding jacket, which has built-in amor and is made to take the brunt of a slide.

Finally, I come to a stop. People are crowding around. For a minute or two, I don't move. There's a burning sensation in my legs and feet, but I'm not screaming so it must not be too bad. I try moving different parts of my body. *Feet, check. Arms and legs, check.*

I think I just got really lucky. I sit up and take my helmet off. Later, I'll notice that my helmet looks like someone pounded on it with a hammer. If I hadn't been wearing it, my face would have looked like ground beef.

I must look terrible because I can see the fear in everyone's eyes. Somebody calls an ambulance. The lady who was driving the car that hit me is freaking out. *Why are you crying? I'm the one who's in pain and just had my baby smashed up. You're fine!* She's pacing back and forth with her hands on her head, muttering over and over again, "Oh my God, oh my God, oh my God."

Weirdly, I'm the one who starts to calm her down. "Do you have insurance?" I ask her, from my position in a gory heap on the ground.

"What? Yes!" she shrieks.

"Then you don't need to worry," I tell her. "Everything's going to work out just fine." This is possibly not the most believable pep talk, given as it's coming from a stunned and bleeding crash victim, but I'm trying. Also, I'm probably in shock.

I don't remember the trip to the hospital, but I know a doctor checked me out, and gave me an IV with morphine. Then he started digging the gravel out of my legs. At that point the morphine stopped working, so I asked for more. They said they gave me more, but I'm sure they were lying.

They didn't even put me to sleep! I mean, *what the hell!* I not only had to feel them digging into my legs but I also had to watch them do it. I swear I think the doctor was enjoying himself. It was like he was digging for gold. Every time he pulled out a rock he'd hold it up, look at it, and smile. Plus I think those nurses were cheering him on. "Come on, deeper. You can find more!" Every time I grimaced in pain, one of those nurses would mark it down. I think they had a bet on how many times they could make me flinch. By the time the doctor finally finished digging, my legs had so many holes in them they looked Swiss cheese.

I knew my foot was going to be bad. I'd felt the pain as I was skidding across the pavement. I'd felt it when the road had finally worn through my boot and started attacking the flesh underneath. I'd tried to shift my weight off my foot, but that just made it worse for my legs. I could feel the layers of flesh being pulled away with every second my body was in motion. I'm surprised the doctors didn't see bone. Maybe they did and just kept it from me. They carefully cut the boot away, then they cut off the bloody sock. I had had enough by this point and closed my eyes, trying to think of something else. *Anything else.* After what felt like hours of agonizing pain, they finally had my foot wrapped up and the doctors were done.

Despite the fiery torment up my right leg and foot, I got lucky. None of my bones were broken, but the pain of the accident didn't end with the physical. My buddies Jose, Boyd, and Brian came to take me home from the hospital, and when they walked into my room and saw at all the bandages I was wrapped in, did they express sympathy? Horror? An ounce of compassion?

"Look, it's Mummy Boy," jeered Jose, and they all burst out laughing.

And the next day HR called to tell me I was unemployed.

HEADED TO SWITZERLAND

It took about ten months, but I finally found a job with SAF, a company that develops software that forecasts demand for all the stuff you buy in a store. You know, stuff: like new Harleys, Honda Civics, and lengths of gauze after the doctor's finished picking gravel out of your leg. I had to take a cut in pay, but at least the job was in my field. And to make things more interesting, the company's headquarters was 5,396 miles away. In Switzerland.

At first, that didn't seem important. Abstract, even. But it sure didn't stay abstract for long.

My coworker Paul and I were part of a bigger team that was headquartered in Switzerland, along with our boss, Caroline. One day I was on the phone with her and she said, "I think you should meet the team in person."

I was like, "That sounds like a good idea."

"Would you like to come to Switzerland for a week?"

Say what? I try to remain calm. "If you think that would help us to work better, I guess I can come to Switzerland."

Three weeks later, I was on a plane.

I arrived in Zurich and took a train to Tägerwilen, feeling like a kid mesmerized by the scenery as I traveled across the Swiss countryside. The beauty was beyond any storybook I'd ever seen. Mountains, trees, rivers, fields with cows *actually wearing Swiss cowbells*. Every so often, our immaculate train would pull into a small town for a minute to let people on and off. As we neared Tägerwilen, I could finally see Lake Constance. It was so big and blue, with Switzerland, Austria, and the Alps on one side, Germany on the other. When I arrived at the station, several of my colleagues were there, waiting for me. They helped me get checked into my hotel, and later that evening they took me to dinner. Every step of the way, someone was by my side, always ready to help.

When I walked into the office the next morning, my co-workers greeted me. Too much to see and do in just a week. I really hoped I would get to go back someday to visit again. Little did I know I would get more than a visit.

* * *

After about a year and a half, SAF got bought out by a German multinational called SAP that had a large office in Zurich. (I know, these guys aren't big on whimsical company names.) And as a part of the transition period, someone from human resources Switzerland came to see us.

"Ve are a team!" he insisted, in his German-accented English. "Ve are a family! *Everyone* vill be an equal! *Everyone* vill have ze same opportunities in zis new structure!"

I raised my hand. He didn't looked thrilled about it, but he nodded his head. "Yes?"

"I appreciate the sentiment, but that's not true," I pointed out, trying to keep it professional.

The HR dude looked pained. "*Vat* is not true?"

"Well, the job postings with the new company structure. Some of them are translated into English, but some are just written in German."

He raised one eyebrow and made a sort of clucking noise in the back of his throat. "Zees jobs are ze ones zat will not interest you."

"But one *does* interest me. It's for a product manager, only I can't read any of the details in German."

His nostrils flared. "And zees interests you?"

I nodded.

"You are *sure* it interests you?"

I nodded again. "Yeah. I mean, yes, in fact that's what I used to do, a couple years back."

He sniffed. The next day, he interviewed me. And apparently I didn't completely suck, because a few weeks later I was having a video interview with someone from Switzerland, and soon enough, I was on a plane to Europe.[1]

Next thing I knew, they offered me the job. I had a few months to get my affairs in order and move across the ocean.

---

1   Look, German accents are funny, but that dialogue wasn't exactly accurate. In reality, most of the people in my company spoke British English, and they usually spoke it better than me.

COWBOY

So I didn't actually go to Switzerland by myself.

I'd adopted Cowboy from a rescue about 6 years previously. One day, I woke up and said to myself, *I want a dog.*

When I came across Cowboy on the rescue shelter website, I was certain he was the dog for me. I went to the shelter and made arrangements to pick him up. And as fate would have it, I adopted him on my birthday—so each year, we celebrate everything all at once. We always celebrate big.

Cowboy's most distinguishing feature is that he has one blue eye and one brown one. When we got home from the shelter, he immediately started exploring the house. I just wanted to pet him, but as I raised my hand, he cowered away. *Poor guy.* Later, I made a sudden movement near him and he jumped. I had to slow down and find out what he was okay with. He loved a belly rub, but not being put on his back. I could touch him anywhere but his paws. One day when cooking, I dropped a pan from the counter crashed to the floor. This sent Cowboy sprinting to a corner to hide. It was fun to watch the change in him over the years, though. More tail wags and less shrinking away in fear. Soon, when I made a sudden noise, he'd run to me to make sure I was okay. We became best friends, a pack of two.

At the time of the adoption, I lived alone in an older three-bedroom house with a large, fenced-in backyard. Even though I was single and not dating at the time, I purchased the bigger house because I thought it would make a better investment if I wanted to sell it later. It turned out the three bedrooms were perfect. One was my master bedroom, the second was for my parents when they visited, and the third one made a nice little office.

I added some doggy doors to the setup, and Cowboy could go outside and play or do his business any time he wanted. But one morning, I saw him lying in the bedroom, staring out the window at a tree in our backyard.

"What are you doing, Cowboy?" I asked. "You know how to use your doggy door."

That's when his ears perked up. Something had his attention. I walked over to see what he was looking at. *A squirrel.* At that moment, the squirrel jumped from the tree to the ground. Before I could react, Cowboy sprang up and knocked me out of the way, barreling full-speed toward the back door. I could hear his claws tearing into the carpet as he scrambled to get outside. I steadied myself and looked out the window, only to see a cloud of grass and dust as Cowboy tore around the corner of the house toward his prey. Luckily for the squirrel, he reacted in time and leapt up to safety. Cowboy bounded to the tree and scrabbled at the bark, doing his best to climb up after the squirrel. Then he started circling the tree with his tail wagging in the air, delighted for the chase. After a while, he trotted back into the house and went back to his window.

Sure enough, soon the squirrel came down again—and Cowboy was off to the races. As many times as he tried he never did get the squirrel, but he sure had fun working on it. And when Cowboy was in hunter mode, I just learned to stay out of his way.

Before Cowboy, I used to let work define me. If I had a bad day at work, I had a bad day at home. If work was stressful, I was stressed. One night, I remember coming home in a bad mood. I came up the driveway and pulled inside the garage to park.

By the time I got out of the car, Cowboy had already sprinted to the garage and was waiting to greet me. Wagging his tail, running in circles—his excitement was intoxicating. How can you stay mad after that kind of greeting?

I'll tell you what: you can't. Cowboy just made me happy.

Later on that night, I got an upsetting email from work. Cowboy noticed and immediately grabbed his stuffed squirrel, trying to get me to play with him.

"Go away, Cowboy," I growled, scowling at my screen.

Did I mention my dog is stubborn? He would *not* pay attention. Somehow, he scooted his way onto my lap, until he'd shoved that stuffed squirrel in my face.

"Go AWAY, Cowboy!" I yelled, losing my patience this time. "Can't you see I DON'T WANT TO PLAY?"

But he wouldn't. And eventually, I started to play. Before long I was laughing and having a good time and completely forgot about work or that stupid email.

It's not just about the stuffed squirrel, though. Cowboy also saved my life.

I've suffered from depression for years, and one day, not long after adopting Cowboy, I had a bad day. I could feel something was off. It was peaceful and quiet. No neighbors making any noise. It was a Saturday, and no one was outside mowing or doing any work. It was still and ominous. I got myself a brandy and decided to relax on the couch.

It's amazing how the mind works when you're depressed. It pulls you in. All you can think about is what the depression allows. It's like a demon that has possessed you and controls all your thoughts. That day, it whispered in my ear, *Have another drink. Remember all these bad things. Remember how they happened this way.*

The demon was lying, but that didn't matter. You couldn't even tell it was a demon. It looked so professional. Perfectly dressed. I could see my reflection in its smile and a twinkle in its eyes. It could be my best friend. The demon twisted and presented the memories how it wanted me to remember them. *Have another drink,* it said. *Forget about your family; forget about your friends. Only think about me and what I'm telling you.*

Have another drink... think about how bad life is and will always be. Think of nothing else, just me.

Have another drink. It's not worth it. Everyone would be better off with you dead.

Have another drink; you'll finally find peace and never be in pain again.

Focus on me...

Have another drink; think of nothing but what I tell you.

Have another drink. Remember that gun your dad gave you, the beautiful Smith and Wesson 9mm?

It's in your room.

Let's have another drink and go look at it.

It's so peaceful, so calm.

Such a good day to die.

Listen to me, the demon continued, *Have another drink.*

Is it loaded? Good. Have one last drink for the road. It's time to sleep, to feel no more pain. It's all right; you deserve the rest. The world is terrible and will never be better. Listen to me; relax.

Focus on me, nothing else. Don't think, only me. It's so quiet, such a good time to end it all. Let's sit down on the bed with the gun. That's good, raise the gun to your head.

I hesitated, but it was sitting next to me, helping me. It raised my arm for me.

Nice and easy. There you go. Put the barrel against your head, it said and guided the gun to my temple. *Now squeeze the trigger. Nice and easy, almost there.* I could feel it, helping me. Holding the gun. It slowly wrapped my finger around the trigger. It told me not to worry; it was there to help me. We started to squeeze.

Right then, Cowboy bounded in. He looked up at me and started barking like a maniac.

He shattered my concentration and I stopped squeezing the trigger.

"Goddamnit, Cowboy!" I snarled.

Get him out of here now. You have something you must finish, the demon whispered. I lowered the gun so I could yell at Cowboy and chase him away, then finish what my thoughts were telling me.

I never got a chance to yell.

The moment I lowered the gun, Cowboy leapt on the bed and started licking my face. That was all it took to break the spell. With every kiss from Cowboy, the demon lost more and more of its power. Its shape changed from a human friend to the demon it was. Claws replaced hands. Its face became leathery and grotesque.

It became angry and through its pointed teeth it was shouting, "Get rid of the dog, get rid of the dog!" But it was too late. I was focused on Cowboy now. The demon fled.

Chased away by the love of a dog.

Sitting on my bed with Cowboy, I couldn't believe what I'd been about to do. When you're in that state of mind, you don't think about anything. Not your friends, your family, the consequences, or your dog. What would have happened to Cowboy if I'd pulled that trigger? He would have been all alone. Sure, my parents or sister would have taken him—Cowboy was my child and they wouldn't have let anything happen to him, but they could never have loved and spoiled him like I did. I know he would have missed me.

I made a promise at that moment. I told him that as long as he lived, I would not only never try to take my life again, but I would actively try to stay alive. There have been many times since that day when the demon has whispered in my ear.

Every time he did, I said, "Not today, Demon. I made a promise to Cowboy."

ALARM BELLS

When I first arrived in Switzerland, all I had with me was a suitcase and a dog. The company rented me a nice apartment in a small village near the office, and when I say small, I mean SMALL. Not only this village didn't have a Walmart, it didn't have a grocery store. It did have one small shop where you could buy a few items like bread, but it was closed most of the time during the winter.

On the other hand, Gottlieben was a beautiful hamlet, right on Lake Constance. You could walk from one end to the other in five minutes. Most of the narrow roads were paved with old cobblestones, and trees lined the path along the lake. Walking Cowboy was great because we left the house and within minutes we were outside the village, on a dirt trail in the country. My apartment was right next to an old church. I could walk for two minutes and be at a coffeeshop by the lake. Cowboy and I would visit on nice days, sitting outside to enjoy a coffee and a treat.

My rental wasn't exactly private. The owner lived downstairs, and we shared an entrance. But there was a nice balcony, and the apartment was fully furnished. Unfortunately, I was kind of stuck there: legally, I wasn't allowed to go to the office.

That was a temporary situation due to issues with my work visa, but it was still pretty isolating. It was November and the village had closed for the winter. It felt like I was living in a ghost town. So: new country, no people, no contacts. It seemed like Cowboy and I were shipwrecked on a deserted island. But at least we were having an adventure.

Here in Switzerland, Cowboy and I no longer had a backyard. Now I had to put him on a leash and take him out for walks just so he could do his business. Rain, wind, sleet, or snow. Four times a day I put a leash on him and took him for a walk. Did I mention that I had to pay a dog tax? That's right, in Switzerland (and other European countries) you pay a tax for every dog you own. It sounds unfair at first, but there's a great reason. The first time Cowboy and I were walking around, we came across these little poop stations. They had a compartment that contained unused doggy poop bags to take, and a compartment to put your full doggy poop bags. That's what the dog tax pays for. You better use them too, because they have people who patrol the parks and if you get caught not picking up your dog's poop, you can get hit with a hefty fine. I was also told that anyone could report you. The poop patrol didn't even need to see it happen—they took the poop crime on faith.

Cowboy and I both enjoyed walking . I learned that going for a walk is about more than just pooping. It's a bonding experience. Back in Texas, I always played with him. We chased each other and caught balls in the backyard; I shared my dinners with him; I cooked him steaks... but it wasn't until we started walking in Switzerland that we fully cemented our friendship.

Then there were the church bells.

I don't know about you, but growing up in Texas I didn't hear many church bells. As a matter of fact, I think the only time I heard any at all was when I was watching TV or the movies—especially Old Westerns. If a building caught fire, the church bells started ringing, and then all the towns-folk would rush in to help put out the blaze. They'd form a bucket brigade from the town well to the fire. That was *my* idea of church bells: they always signaled an emergency.

On one of my first days in Switzerland, I was relaxing in my apartment. Cowboy was dozing next to me, and we were both very peaceful. Next thing I knew, church bells started clanging.

I shot up in bed. *Holy crap, something's on fire!*

I rushed outside to join the fight, almost tripping and falling down the stairs in my haste. *Where is it?!* I kept thinking. I started running around town, frantically looking for the fire. *Why aren't people rushing out of their houses to help? Everyone must be able to hear the bells. Why am I the only one freaking out? My God people, there's a fire somewhere and no one cares!*

After a few minutes of not seeing or smelling any smoke, I start to slow down. *Hmmm, maybe there IS no fire after all?* That is when I calmed down enough to really take a look at all the people around me. They kept looking at me and whispering. Then I got close enough to hear what they were saying. I couldn't understand everything, but I sure got the part about "crazy American."

I walked around town one last time to make sure. On my way home, I tapped an older gentleman on the shoulder. "Was there a fire anywhere?" I asked, hesitantly.

"No" he replied, looking at me funny.

"But what about all those bells?"

"The church bells, you mean?" he asked, amused. "They're ringing the hour. It was twelve noon."

"Just twelve noon?"

"Yes," he nodded. "And they will ring again at one o'clock." Then he smiled and walked away, kind of shaking his head.

Eventually, I learned church bells ring constantly in Europe. As a matter of fact, they ring every hour, on the hour, usually on the half hour, and also on Sundays.

Did I mention my apartment was right next to a church?

CRACK DRUGS

Where's the bucket? There's no way I'm making it to the restroom.

My head is pounding and I can barely move. I bend over and retch into a trashcan. I'm shaking uncontrollably; I'm so cold and yet I'm sweating profusely.

This is miserable. I've only been here about a week and I'm already going to die. Maybe I'm allergic to Switzerland? How long will it take them to find my body? I wonder how bad it will smell by the time they find it. What am I going to do about Cowboy? If I die, who will take care of him?

I force myself to sit up. *How can something as tiny as bacteria make my body hurt so badly?* I stand, leaning against the wall to keep from falling over.

The room will not stop spinning. I stagger to the table where I keep my laptop. With each step, my head is on the verge of exploding. The pressure is immense, but I need to let someone know that I'm dying so they'll come and take care of Cowboy.

I make it to the table and sit down. Luckily my computer is on already and I just need to bring up the email. *Good Lord, I can barely think. This is the worst fever I can ever remember.* I focus to make my computer stop spinning. I start to type out an email to Christoph, my new boss:

If no one hears from me in a few days I will be dead. Send someone over to get my dog.

I'm about to click Send when I consider that maybe my fever is causing me to be a tad melodramatic. I decide to delete the email. Instead, I decide that what I really need to do is fill up dozens of water bowls so Cowboy has plenty to drink.

"You can eat my body, Buddy," I tell him. "But only if you get really hungry."

I fill up eight bowls of water and four coffee mugs and arrange them all over the floor, then I have to go back to bed. I stumble back to the bedroom, shaking violently. *Oh, you soft warm covers, come to me and wrap me in your delicious embrace.*

A few hours later, I wake up again. *You need medicine. Why didn't you bring any, idiot?* Of course, it wasn't unreasonable to assume I could always buy medicine in Switzerland, but now that seems like a deadly mistake. *Is there even a grocery store here?*

I consider emailing someone at work to ask for help, but then I remember the melodramatic dog-rescue note and I think better of it. I also need to take Cowboy for a walk. He's been sniffing around the corners of the apartment, and I can tell he's getting ready to pee on the floor. He's staring at the door, focused on it like it's some kind of a squirrel. I realize he's giving me one last warning that I better put his harness on and take him out that door or he will use it like the tree it came from.

I make it out of bed and pull on my shoes, then open the door and stagger outside. *Dead man walking.* Now I need to get down the stairs. Holding onto the railing, I take one step and then one more. Cowboy is being patient because he knows I'm dying.

Outside on the street, there are normal people walking. They take one look at me and hurry to the other side of the street. I'm hunched over, holding my head with one hand and the leash with the other. Every cough is like someone hitting me over the head with a sledgehammer. We finally make it to the grass and Cowboy joyfully relieves himself.

I have never been so happy for my dog to poop.

A couple of days pass and I amaze myself by not dying. I start to put away the extra bowls of water lying around, and the apartment looks less like the home of a crazy person.

Now it's time to go find some medicine. Cowboy and I walk to the gas station, thinking we can at least get some cough medicine and some ibuprofen. The walk is exhausting, but the promise of drugs motivates me to keep going. We finally arrive and I go in to claim my prize. I know that I won't be able to read the label, but I figure I can guess what it is, based on the picture. I mean, even if I accidentally eat rat poison I won't feel worse than I have the past few days.

I hurry up and down the aisles, looking for bottle with a picture of a sick person on it. *Nope.* I slow down for Round Two and carefully scan all the items. *Still nope. This stinks.* Okay, for Round Three I scrutinize every item and try to determine if it might be medicine. *Nothing, nichts. Total strike out.*

I leave dejected. *Now what am I going to do?*

Eventually, I do find a grocery store. I leave Cowboy out front in the shade with water and a treat to chew on. This time though, I'm feeling good. I just know success is at my fingertips. As I walk in the front door I'm trying to visualize where I would be if I was medicine. I am on a mission. I sweep the store.

No drugs, dammit.

Why the heck fire do they make it so hard to find medicine in this country?

In the US I can walk into any grocery store or gas station and at least grab an aspirin. Here I can't find jack.

I'm desperate now. I look around frantically to ask someone for help. I've been working on my German, so I know enough to be able to say "Excuse me," and "I need help." I'm wandering up and down the aisles, trying to gain some confidence to ask someone, when I run into a little old lady pushing a shopping cart.

"Entschuldigen Sie," I say, tentatively. *"Ich brauche bitte Hilfe,"* And then that's the end of my German. *Now what?* "Uh, do you speak English?" I ask.

The lady shakes her head. *"Nein."*

"I NEED TO BUY MEDICINE," I shout, because of course talking louder makes everyone magically understand English.

Then I try mixing the two languages. "WO IST DAS MEDICINE?" This makes no sense in either language, and the lady looks at me like I have lost my mind.

Okay, yelling doesn't help. "Medicine...drugs?" I venture.

"Drugs?" she repeats.

Sounding like a maniac, I cheer, "YES DRUGS!"

Now she looks suspicious. *"Wo ist das drugs?"* she wants to know. "No drug. Amsterdam, not Switzerland."

Oh God. She thinks I'm hunting for drug drugs. Like crack drugs. I decide to cut my losses and go home.

Later, I learn that in Switzerland and Germany they don't sell over-the-counter drugs in grocery stores or gas stations. The only place you can find them is at an *Apotheke*. Which is great, except I still don't know how to pronounce it.

I take a train to Konstanz (Constance in US), determined not to fail. Konstanz is a larger town located nearby, just across the border in Germany. Most Swiss people living near the border go into Konstanz to shop because the prices are cheaper than Switzerland. On the weekend, traffic is always backed up at the border from all the shoppers from Zurich. Because of this, you have a plethora of places to shop. I walk up to the first younger person I see.

"Do you speak English?" I ask.

He replies, "Yes, can I help you."

I felt like hugging him. *Finally, someone who speaks English! I should be able to find the medicine I need.* I still want to use the right word, though. "Where is the A-pothicky?" I ask, with the "th" sounding like "the."

He looks at me with a bewildered expression and shakes his head. "Sorry, I don't know where that is."

Damn. Did I misunderstand? I walk away quickly, my head hung low. Then I try the next young person I see. "Can you please tell me where the A-pothicky is"?

Just like that, her smile evaporates. "No," she says, and walks away.

I feel like crying. *How can it be so hard to find an aspirin? Do Germans not get headaches? Alright, one more try.*

"Excuse me, can you help me please?" I stammer at a man about my age.

"I can try." My desperation must be showing, because this guy looks sympathetic. "What do you need?"

I can't look him in the eye. With my head hung low, I rush out the words. "Can you help me find an A-pothicky"?

Here it is, the puzzled look in the eyes, the weird expression in the face. "Sorry, I beg your pardon?"

Finally, I blurt it out. "I need a place to buy aspirin and cough medicine."

He bursts out laughing. "Oh, you mean an app-O-Tech-Kay."

"YES!" I holler. "An app-O-Tech-Kay, app-O-Tech-Kay!"

I look around and see that people are stopping and staring because I'm jumping up and down and screaming, so I calm down a little. "Can you show me where one is?" I ask, a big grin on my face.

"Sure," he beckons. "Follow me." And we skip down the road together, on our merry way to the Apotheke.

After spending a small fortune buying a drug for every possible thing that could ever happen to me, I fill my backpack with my treasure and head back home. Now that I'm aware of them, I see these magical shops on almost every corner. As I go past one I smile and call out, "Look, it is an "APP-o-tech-kay! Hey! it's another app-o-tech-KAY!"

Man, those people must have thought I was nuts.

FILET MIGNON

When I first moved to Switzerland, finding drugs was the least of my problems. At first, I couldn't even find food. I eventually located a gas station that had a couple of shelves full of products that *looked* like food, but I couldn't read any German and I couldn't be sure.

Just as I was leaving, I spied something in the corner that saved me: a small shelf, loaded with fresh bread.

This meant I would not die by starvation in Switzerland. For many days, like a condemned prisoner, I ate bread and drank water for every meal.

Have you ever had a good steak? I mean a *really* good steak. Pink, juicy, melts in your mouth, just the right seasoning. I'm getting hungry just thinking about it. Can you imagine eating nothing but plain bread? Let me tell you, you start to miss steak. You start to *dream* of steak. *Oh how badly you want a steak.* I believe a diet of bread and water can cause hallucinations. One afternoon I thought I heard Cowboy say "moo."

That day, Cowboy and I headed to the gas station for our daily loaf of bread. It was busy, so I walked around playing my new favorite game, which was "Guess what this weird Swiss product is." Based on the pictures, I think they had a lot of things you'd expect to find at a gas station. They had what looked like car oil, and something else that may have been window defroster. They also had a large cold section dedicated to different beers.

Suddenly, at the end of an aisle, I spotted it. I couldn't believe my eyes. I think I heard angels singing. It was sitting there, on the shelf. It was not bread; it was a wonderful treasure, and it was all for me. I grabbed it before someone else could. I hastened to the cash register, afraid they wouldn't sell it to me. The person at the counter scanned my items and I read the price on the register. I handed him my money, seized my prize, and scurried out the door.

As soon as I got home, I began to prepare my feast. I was drooling. Cowboy was drooling. He wouldn't leave my side. I almost stepped on him a couple of times as I was fixing dinner. He was making sure that I was going to share my bounty with him.

Before long, it was ready. So much anticipation. It was hot, with just the right seasoning. I took a bite. *Oh my God. This is amazing.* It was the best thing ever. It was better than steak. It had to be a filet mignon or something. *This is the best steak I have ever eaten.*

I gave a bite to Cowboy. He almost took my finger off trying to tear it from my hand. After we finished eating, I leaned back in my chair, fully sated. It was one of the best dinners of my life. I got up and started cleaning up the dishes.

It was then that I put it together. That wasn't a steak.

I just ate a can of Raviolios.

Obviously, I knew the stuff in a can wasn't a steak, but let me tell you: that was the greatest can of Raviolios I have ever eaten.

When I started searching for my permanent apartment, a nearby grocery store was a major requirement. This was something I'd never considered in the States. Growing up in the US, food was just always there. Of course, Switzerland has just as much food as the US; I just couldn't find it right away. That made a big impression on me. And the other thing that made an impact? Learning how to say "Where is the grocery store?" in German. Let me tell you, I picked that one up quick.

NO SACKS

Then one day, I found the mother lode.

It took me awhile to venture off the main paths because I was terrified of getting lost. I didn't have a cell phone yet, and I didn't know where to buy a map. Not being able to read or speak German made me nervous that if I did get lost, I would never be able to find my way back. Instead I would wander the cobblestone streets with Cowboy, growing weaker and weaker, as I mumbled the few German phrases I knew: *sprechen sie Englisch*, and *guten morgen*. Eventually, they'd find out skeletonized bodies, abandoned in a ditch.

Besides, by that point I was running low on toilet paper. And that can make a guy a little nervous.

I guess my desperation made me bold. So one day I left the safety of the lake and decided to head up the hill.

Cowboy and I passed the train station, the furthest we'd ventured since arriving in Switzerland. We came to an unfamiliar area with mysterious buildings on either side. *Are they shops or are they houses?* Honestly, I had no idea. It can be really hard to tell the difference in Europe.

Eventually, we arrived in a larger town, called Tägerwilen. Now hunger was fueling our odyssey. We passed a post office, an office building, and suddenly there it was, on the left: a grocery store. Actually it was fairly modest, but after shopping in a gas station, it looked like paradise on Earth.

I skipped to the front door, tied Cowboy up under some shade, and gave him a treat and some water. Then I hustled over to the shopping carts, eager to load up on food and supplies. I grabbed the shopping cart and pulled...It wouldn't come out.

What the...is it stuck?

I tugged on the shopping cart in the next lane over. That one wouldn't come out either. And that's when I noticed: *the shopping carts were all chained together.* I figured the store must be closed, so I started to walk away.

As I went to get Cowboy, a car pulled into the parking lot. A middle-aged man got out, helped himself to a cart, and went inside the store.

What the heck??? Now I HAD to know the truth.

So, I waited for another car. This time I stood next to the carts, trying to look cool and not creepy as I watched. It turns out, *these crazy Swiss people were putting a coin in a slot to open the lock and release the cart.*

Well, I thought to myself, *there's no way I'M going to pay to use a shopping cart to buy my groceries.* I was filled with righteous indignation. Even though I wanted to fill a cart to the top with groceries, I rejected it on principle. Instead, I grabbed a handbasket.

I walked up and down the aisle, feasting my eyes on all the wonderful food products. I didn't know what everything was, but I could take a pretty good guess. Canned food has pictures on it. Toilet paper is obvious. A dead chicken looks like a dead chicken, whether you're in Texas or Switzerland. Of course fruits were easy but they also had a lot of veggies

I didn't recognize. In the end, meat is meat, but they had some things in the meat department that even had this Texas boy a little worried. Not a lot of beef, but about every type of sausage you could imagine, including ones made with blood and calf's liver. I carefully picked out the items that would get me through the afternoon and made plans to come back later for more. I figured I could easily manage a couple of sacks of groceries on each trip.

In line to pay, I got nervous because I was afraid I'd have to make conversation with the checkout lady. But the good news is, she had zero desire to talk to me. I put my groceries on a conveyor belt and the cashier took each one and scanned it. But then something changed. She didn't put the groceries in a bag. She didn't even reach for a bag. My groceries just piled up on the other side of her.

Um. Maybe I have to bag my own groceries? I looked around for sack to put them in.

NO SACKS.

Now I was panicking. *What am I supposed to do?* I furtively scanned the next lane over and saw that those people had brought their own bags. *Crap. What do I do?*

The checkout lady finished scanning all my items, and then she started talking to me in German. She sounded annoyed.

"*Sprechen sie Englisch?*" I ventured. "*Guten morgen?*"

She shook her head in frustration and pointed to the total on her register. At least numbers were the same in German. Now the people behind me in line were looking agitated. I was sure they all figured I was a stupid American, and I couldn't say they were wrong.

But I didn't want to look stupid. I pretended that I knew exactly what was going on and what I was supposed to do.

I calmly took my money out and gave the lady a big bill, so I could avoid having to do math in German. She thrust my change at me and turned to the next customer, and then I had to figure out what to do with my groceries.

I put my money away and gathered up all my supplies in my arms. Looking like a circus clown act, I stumbled out to where Cowboy was, put everything down, untied his leash, and picked everything up again. There I was, walking down the street with my arms full of groceries, when all of a sudden Cowboy stopped and his ears perked up.

"Cowboy, no" I said in a panicked tone, fearing what would come next. I looked down at him and followed his stare.

"No buddy, don't do it."

I followed his gaze across the field and there it was, his first Swiss squirrel.

"Oh God Cowboy, no, not now!"

But it was inevitable. He took off in a full charge and he was dragging me with him, groceries flying everywhere.

"Cowboy, STOP!"

You can't stop a train that easy. Cowboy was now dragging me across the field, hands full, groceries flying everywhere. Yet again, people were staring at me. *There goes that crazy American again.*

Cowboy finally got the squirrel treed and he stopped long enough for me to gain control. After he lost interest in his prey, we headed back toward the road, stopping along the way to gather all the grocery items I'd dropped.

Somehow we made it back to the apartment with all that food.

I later learned that those other shoppers weren't paying for their shopping carts, after all. It's just a deposit, and you get your coin back when you bring back the cart. Also, you're supposed to bring your own shopping bags when you go to the store (or if you speak German, you can buy a bag.)

So eventually, I got wise. I bought a backpack that I always wore when I went out walking with Cowboy. That way I could stop at the store and fill it up. Every Saturday, we'd walk to the grocery store, I'd fill up my backpack, and then we'd head home. They even had a small doggy section and I made sure to get Cowboy an extra special treat each week. And every so often, I'd pick up a can of Raviolios—just to check if it still tasted like steak.

SECRET SOCIETY

Everyone knows that Europe is full of secret societies, especially Switzerland with all of its shadowy anonymous bank accounts. But what I didn't realize is that the secret societies don't just run the world—they also run the trash collection.

In order to get your trash picked up in Switzerland, it is not enough to be a person who resides in a house or an apartment. First, you must be admitted into the Super Secret Swiss Trash Society. This was my first foray into the undercover world of secret societies. It took me weeks to pass their tests, and until I decoded their mysteries, I was condemned to live in a house full of trash.

EPISODE 1: IN SEARCH OF RELIEF

Long about Week Two of my residence in Switzerland, my garbage was starting to pile up and smell. I knew I had to act quickly or I would soon be confronted with a health hazard.

Little did I know, they were watching me. And the game had only just begun.

At first, I innocently applied the US Apartment Strategy. Based on my experience of living in my own apartment in the United States, I reasoned that I must have access to a building trash bin.

This proved totally naïve.

I went outside and walked around my building. I did not find any trash bins. I decided to dig a bit deeper and I searched the garage, the basement, and even the communal garden. No trash bins. I even walked around to other apartment buildings, thinking I could "borrow" one of theirs until I could figure out where mine was.

No luck: Switzerland 1, Randy 0.

EPISODE 2: THE MISSION

The odor is getting worse. I must break the code and learn the secrets of the trash.

This time I decided to try The US House Strategy. When I had a house in the US, I would put my trash out next to the curb on trash day and it would magically disappear by the time I got home. So logically, all I needed to do was figure out what day was trash day.

Cowboy and I embarked on a mission: every morning, we got up early and walked around looking for trash bags. Finally, one morning I spotted them.

HA! I thought to myself. *I have your secret now! I shall get my trash picked up with everyone else.* Cowboy and I rushed back to the house, I gathered up all my bags, and I set them down next to the curb. I wanted to make *sure* I had them out before the trashman came.

Mission accomplished, we had a pleasant breakfast and then we went out to the park. Walking home, I notice that all the trash bags I'd seen earlier were gone. "You see,

Cowboy?" I remarked with pride. "All it took was a little American know-how."

Then I got to my place. There, where I left them, were my bags. All the other bags were gone, but not mine. *Damn. This is going to be a harder mystery to solve than I thought. I must discover the secret quickly or I may die in a pile of trash.*

Current Score: Switzerland 2, Randy 0.

EPISODE 3: THE DECODER RING

There was only one possible explanation. Clearly, the Swiss had a secret code that allowed them to be detected as members of the secret society so that their bags were picked up.

It was time to go undercover.

The next trash day, Cowboy and I pretended to go for a walk. As I approached the first set of trash bags, I pretended to tie my shoe as I inspected the bags for some sort of hidden communication.

HA! My undercover work paid off. The Super Secret Swiss Trash Society had super secret Swiss stickers on them to show membership. The trashman must have had a decoder ring to know which bags to pick up.

I had to be sure, so Cowboy and I continued our undercover surveillance. We went to multiple bags and noticed that smaller bags had one sticker, and the larger bags had two stickers.

This is it! I have discovered the secret. I will get my trash picked up next week as part of the initiation, and then I, too, will be a member of the Super Secret Swiss Trash Society.

That very day Cowboy and I headed out to get our stickers. I'd done my research. I'd used Google translate to find out how to say "trash" and "sticker" in German. And it worked! I got my stickers. I went home and put three stickers on each bag, just to make sure.

EPISODE 4: A NEW HOPE

The next week, Cowboy and I carefully planned our moves to make sure the trash was picked up. I knew that The Super Secret Swiss Trash Society would do everything in its power to stop me from becoming a member, so I had to be prepared. My guess was that they would have the trash man come earlier than usual and I would miss him.

Ha! I'm smarter than that. I set my alarm extra early and Cowboy and I got up at oh-dark-thirty. We were ready. Today was going to be the day of initiation. We decided to sneak our bags out to make sure that no one could try and stop us.

Then we decided to go into Konstanz to get some special treats to celebrate our success. We walked home with our heads held high. We had done it.

As I rounded the corner to our residence, I expected to be greeted by several figures wearing dark hooded robes. They would ceremonially offer a robe to me, and congratulate me for passing their trials.

Instead, I saw my trash bags sitting there.

How? Why? It's trash day; I HAVE THE STICKERS.

Will I ever become a member, or will I die trying, smothered in a pile of my own garbage?

That day, I almost gave up. *Maybe an American just isn't allowed into the Super Secret Swiss Trash Society. Maybe it was my fate to move all the way here just to expire in my own refuse. I'm sorry I let you down, Buddy. It was nice knowing you.*

Just then, Cowboy went over to the sidewalk and peed. There it was, the SECRET BLUE DOT. The last piece of the initiation puzzle. Cowboy peed on it and revealed it to me. *We can still make it; we have not totally failed yet.*

Current Score: Switzerland 3, Randy 0.

EPISODE 5: RETURN OF THE TRASHMAN

One week later. *This is it. We have to make it.*

Cowboy and I got up early again. We planned and we executed. We were determined to make it into our first secret society. Cowboy stood guard as I brought the bags out. I took them to the secret blue dot where Cowboy had marked the spot the week before. I put the bags at the dot and we cautiously retreated inside.

This time, we watched and waited. Time passes slowly when you're waiting for the trashman. We had to do it though. Neither of us felt we could make it another week.

Finally, it happened:

I saw the trashmen coming down the street. They were picking up the other bags. *Here they come, slowly.* They approached my bags. They looked around.

Cowboy and I ducked so we couldn't be seen. I lifted my head up and peeked, just a little. One of them was on a cell phone. *I think they're trying to decide if I've passed all the tests.*

Cowboy started circling the apartment, nervous and unsure. He had found what we thought was the last secret, but would that be enough? I looked up again. The trashmen were still talking. My bags were still there. The tension built.

And then I saw it. They must have gotten permission. One of them bent down and took a bag of my garbage. He lifted it in the air as if he were saluting me in congratulations for being accepted, and then tossed it gracefully into his truck.

Cowboy came over and jumped up on me out of joy. *We did it!* Later that day we go back to Konstanz and I bought Cowboy a German blood sausage, thanking him for his part in helping discover the secrets and gain membership to The Super Secret Swiss Trash Society.

Final Score: Switzerland 3, Randy 1.[2]

---

2   PS. Don't tell them that I have given away the secrets or they may kick me out and I will never have my trash picked up again. By the way, every so often they change the way things are done just to make sure you are current with all the society's rules. For example, at one point they switched from super secret Swiss stickers to super secret Swiss trash bags and you had to buy these special trash bags to get your trash picked up. (To be honest, I like this method. The more trash you use the more you have to pay. This encourages you to have less waste and to recycle more. Kudos to The Super Secret Swiss Trash Society.)

FIRST DAYS

It's finally here. My first day of work in Switzerland!

I can't wait to get to the office. I wake up early and leap out of bed. Cowboy can tell something's different, and he wags his tail like crazy. I take him out for his morning walk and we're both just skipping along. After our walk I take a shower and finish getting ready.

My office is only about a 3-minute walk from where I live. Did you read that? *A three-minute walk from where I live.* All I need to do is cross an open field and I'm at the office. Is that awesome or what?

As I'm walking to work, the morning sun is shining, welcoming me to my new life. I even take out my camera and take a few pictures. I get to the building, walk around to the entrance, and go inside.

There's an elevator in the lobby, but I'm a European now! I bypass the elevator and take the stairs. I open the door and walk in.

No one is there.

I look at my watch. *7:30. Whoops.* I was so excited I left early and no one's in the office yet. BUT! It doesn't not take long until people start showing up. Everyone is friendly and everything is just soooo cool. Someone takes me to my desk. *This desk is awesome. It is the best desk I ever had. This is my first Swiss desk.* I even have my own Swiss chair to sit in. *Could it get any cooler?* I sit down in my Swiss chair at my Swiss desk and start to unpack my backpack. I've brought my laptop from the US. They have a monitor, mouse, and keyboard ready for me to plug my laptop into.

I plug everything in and start up my laptop. I can't wait to impress them with how quickly I can be productive. My laptop starts and prompts me for the password. I use the nice big keyboard and type in my credentials.

ERROR. INCORRECT USERNAME OR PASSWORD.

Ok, calm down, you're just excited and you missed a key or something. I type it in again.

ERROR. INCORRECT USERNAME OR PASSWORD.

Ok, I know that if I have three failures I get locked out. This time I go nice and slow. I feel the keyboard and made sure I hear a click with every keystroke. I know it will work.

ERROR. INCORRECT USERNAME OR PASSWORD. YOU ARE NOW LOCKED OUT OF THE SYSTEM.

My first 15 minutes on the job and I've already locked myself out of my own computer. I have to go to IT to get it unlocked. It turns out, the keyboard they gave me is a German keyboard and my computer's configured for a US keyboard, and the keys are just different enough that I was getting it wrong every time. What a way to start off right!

Luckily, everyone in the office is really cool. Everyone laughs at me, but it isn't a big deal.

But then I start taking German lessons.

My German classes are Monday and Thursday nights at six. Halfway through the class, we all have a break and we walk down to a coffee shop to get a cup of good coffee, then we practice our German while sipping our drinks. When we go to order, the teacher tells us to say, *"Einen Kaffee em Becher bitte."*

So I walk up to the counter and ask for *einen Kaffee em Becher bitte*, and it works! The guy gives me a coffee to go. I'm learning German! The next break I go to the counter and say *einen Kaffee em Becher bitte*, and it still works!

After about a week of doing this, I get cocky and decided to use my new skills elsewhere. Cowboy and I are out walking, and on the way home we stop at a pizza place.

I walk up to the counter with a big smile on my face. *"Einen Pizza em Becher bitte,"* I declare, thinking I just asked for a pizza to go.

The guy behind the counter gives me a weird look. I know I have a Texas accent, but I didn't think it was *that* bad. So I say it again, this time a little louder. *"Einen Pizza em Becher bitte!"*

The guy looks at me like I'm nuts. Now I'm getting nervous. This time, with my head hung low, in a shaky voice, I mumble, *"Einen Pizza em Becher bitte?"*

He stares at me for what feels like an hour and finally he says, "Do you want a pizza?"

Meekly, I reply, "Yes please, to go?"

At my next German class I tell the pizza story to the class and the teacher bursts out laughing. *"Em Becher* does not mean 'to go,' it means 'in a paper cup.'"

"So I didn't ask for a pizza to go?"

"No, Randy! You asked for a pizza in a paper cup!"

Oh. So much for getting cocky in German.

Later that year, I'm having a private lesson in my apartment when my German teacher asks me about Christmas traditions in the US.

You got this Randy, I think to myself. *"Christmas" is "Weihnachten" and "tree" is "Baum".*

I tell her, *"Ich habe ein Weinachstbaum."*

I have a Christmas tree. So far, so good. She smiles happily and I feel fine. Then she asks me in German, "How long do you keep up your Christmas tree?"

"Ein Monat," I tell her. *One month.*

She keeps pushing. "And what do you place under the tree, Randy?"

So I tell her we put presents down there. *"Unter die Baum, ich habe Schinken."*

And that's when it gets weird. *"Schinken unter die Baum?"* she repeats, wrinkling her nose. *"Wie longe?"*

How long do we keep our presents under the tree? Most of the month, obviously. "Meisten die monate." I am *nailing* this conversation. She must be impressed.

"Why?" she asks, looking horrified.

Then it hits me. I told her we put a *Shinken* under our tree for a month. *That's a present, right?* I open my laptop and suddenly realize why she was so grossed-out about all the *Shinken* under the tree and for so long.

Geschenk is a present. *Shinken* means "ham."

PAPERS PLEASE

It was December and I'd been in Switzerland for about six weeks and working in the office for a couple of weeks, when my company invited me to a Christmas party. My first Christmas party in Switzerland! It was going to be held in Konzil Konstanz, and I'd have to take two trains to get there, but that was no problem. I was getting to be an expert by now.

Soon, the day of the party rolled around. After taking Cowboy out for a nice long walk, I showered, shaved, and put on the nicest clothes I had—dark grey slacks and a dress shirt. This was a fancy Christmas dinner so I wanted to look nice. I grabbed my dress coat and walked to the train station, where I would take the train from Tägerwilen/Gottlieben to Kreuzlingen. From there I would switch trains and go to Konstanz. *No problem.*

I got on the train and we'd barely set off when two officers boarded the car. They were in full uniforms, with guns, pepper spray, and batons. These guys were prepared to deal with criminals.

One of them approached me and started speaking in German.

"Um, I'm sorry?" I stammered. "*Tut mir leid aber ich spreche kein Deutsch.*"[3]

Switching to English, she asked for my ticket. *No problem,* I think, *I have it in my coat pocket.*

And I *did* have it in my coat pocket. My *other* coat pocket. Not the dress coat that I was actually wearing.

I started to sweat. *Oh my God, I don't have my pass. Not only am going to miss the Christmas dinner, but they're going to arrest me and send me to jail.* I was still so new here that I wasn't even sure how to contact anyone without looking at my computer.

· *No one will know what happened. I just won't show up to work and I'll be stuck in a jail cell for who knows how long. Who will feed Cowboy?*

I thought it was bad, but then it got worse.

"May I to see your passport?" the officer asked.

Instinctively I reached for my coat pocket, but my passport was next to my rail pass in my other coat. *Oh crap. No rail pass, no passport. They must think I'm a spy. I'm going downtown for sure. I'll probably spend a few months being interrogated, then they'll deport me and ban me from the country for life.*

The officer conferred with her partner, and who could blame her? Obviously they were dealing with a dangerous secret agent. He put his hand on his gun.

Stay calm. Don't make him mad or he might shoot. Should I tell him I'm a member of the Super Secret Swiss Trash Society?

They asked if I had any identification, anything at all. *Yes.* I had my wallet, and in my wallet, I still had my Texas driver's license. The woman took my license and called into headquarters, while her partner kept glaring at me.

---

3   Which means "I do not speak German." Yes, I know, I am very fancy at this point.

Oh God. Now they know I'm from Texas. They probably think I'm packing a six-shooter and I've got a horse parked nearby to escape on.

The partner started to interrogate me. Panicking, I spilled the whole story. "I'm on my way to a Christmas party in Konstanz and we're getting close to Kreuzlingen and I need to get off to switch trains and I don't know where the next stop will be or how to get back to here from there..."

The train ground to a halt, and the lady barked at me to get off. *This is it. The Swiss SWAT team is waiting.*

I got off the train, fully prepared to fall to my knees and put my hands on my head. I looked up for the helicopter that must be circling overhead. Both the officers followed me. *They're making sure I don't run.* I was about to look at my watch to check the time, but I was afraid they would think I was going for a weapon. I decided not to do anything that might make them shoot me. After a few minutes, the lady's radio buzzed.

I was visibly sweating now. I was sure I was in so much trouble.

She turned to me and gave me my license. "*Danke,* Mr. Snow, I haff confirmed you have a rail pass. Do not forget your passport in ze future, as your Texas license is not valid in Switzerland. Now go! Get your train! Ziss is the one you need for Konstanz!"[4]

---

4   Ok, I admit, I embellished this story a lot. They didn't actually have guns. It just FELT like they did because I was scared I would get into trouble. Also they didn't have mace or batons. Actually, they were extremely friendly and helpful. They went out of their way to make sure I didn't miss my stop, and they even made sure I knew how to get to my party from the train station in Konstanz. If someone from Swiss rail ever reads this book, you are all awesome and if you know of some coworkers who had to deal with a crazy Texan sometime around Christmas of 2012, tell them I said thank you.

BANG, BANG

Sometime in January, Cowboy and I moved into the apartment that was going to be our home for the rest of the time we lived in Switzerland. It was a very nice one-bedroom that was a two-minute walk from the park and the lake, and about a five-minute walk from Germany. Plus there was a grocery store nearby! I was thrilled.

My first weekend in my new apartment, I was ready to start hanging decorations on the wall and making my place feel like home. I took out a beautiful, framed piece that my sister made for me, a handmade cross-stitch of my favorite poem, "The Last Corps Trip." I don't think she knows it, but it's one of my most treasured items.

Now, I've hung many items on walls before. I've hung things in apartments; I've hung things in houses; I've even hung things in offices and warehouses. Hanging things is no big deal. I even brought hardware with me from the US so I wouldn't need to try to find it over here in Switzerland.

So I got to work. I measured and figured out exactly where to hang the hook, I placed the nail against the wall, I hit the nail with my hammer—*ting!* The nail came flying back at me and hit me in the face.

What the heck? Okay, no blood no foul. Let's try this again.

I decided to tap the nail in this time instead of driving it in with one blow. *Tap, tap, tap.* Nothing. The nail did not move. *Tap, tap, tap, Tap, TAP!!!* Again, nothing. The nail would not go in.

It turned out that all the walls in my apartment were made of solid concrete. I couldn't believe it. For the first time in my life, I couldn't hang a simple picture on a wall.

Talk about feeling incompetent. It can be very frustrating learning how to do simple things all over again. *Come to think of it, am I even allowed to hang things on the wall? I know drywall. I know how to patch or repair a hole in drywall. What do you do with cement walls?*

The next Monday at work, I talked it over with some of my friends. Once they finished laughing, they explained that it was common to hang things on the concrete wall and that they even make special concrete drills. On Friday I borrowed a drill from my colleague Ingo for the weekend.

That Sunday, Cowboy and I decided to get back to work on decorating. It seemed like a good plan. In the US, Sunday is a day for getting yard work and other chores done around the house. I got up a little later than usual, went for a walk with my buddy, and we had breakfast. I would guess it was around 10:00 in the morning.

I start drilling holes and everything was going great. It was all working just as Ingo told me it would. Maybe I'd even get this project done without any long delays, like I had when trying to join the Super Secret Swiss Trash Society. *One hole done, second hole done, now a third. I'm getting the hang of this!*

I was just starting hole number four when I heard a banging at my door. I stopped drilling and went to open it, wondering who would be visiting me on a Sunday morning.

It was my downstairs neighbor. I had seen her but never talked with her. *Does she want to welcome me to the building?*

She did not want to welcome me to the building. Before I could say hello, she started yelling at me. I had never been yelled at in German before, and this was quite an experience. I had no idea what she was saying, but based on her expression and how loud she was, she was very upset.

"I'm sorry, *ich spreche kein Deutsch!*" I spluttered, trying to get a word in edgewise.

She would not let me get a single word in. She paused for breath, and by the time I opened my mouth to say something, she started yelling again. I was trying to be polite, so I stood there and pretended to listen. She kept yelling and I still had no clue why.

This continued for several minutes. She would stop for a breath and I would try to interject, but she wouldn't let me.

"*ICH SPRECHE KEIN DEUTSCH!*" I finally yelled.

She stopped and looked at me with a mixed expression, a blend of anger, frustration, irritation, plus a dash of realization that the whole time she was yelling I didn't understand a word she was saying.

She quickly composed herself and in broken English, she snapped, "No noise on Sunday."

I thought maybe I just started too early and woke her up, so I asked if I could continue after lunch.

"NO, no noise on Sunday!"

Now I was baffled. "No noise at *all* on Sunday?"

"NO NOISE ON SUNDAY!" Then she turned and walked away.

I stopped drilling. I returned the drill on Monday, and I never did finish hanging everything up on the walls. I think

I was traumatized. A year later, I still had a box of pictures sitting in the basement that had never been unpacked.

I asked friends at work about it and they told me that in Switzerland it's the law that you cannot make noise at all on Sunday, or any day of the week during the lunch hour from 12:00 to 13:00.

And the Swiss are serious about it: they even turn off power to the washers and dryers during the lunch hour, so you can't make any noise doing laundry. I discovered that little fact the first time I had a day off during the week and I was trying throw a load of washing in.

I pushed the button. Nothing happened.

I thought at first I had blown a fuse. I tried resetting all the breakers in my breaker box. Then I went to the maintenance man and had him reset all the switches in my basement. Flipping through my dictionary, I managed to splutter, "fuses, basement, reset," in German. So he shrugged, reset the fuses, and left.

But my washing machine still wouldn't work. *Is it broken? Do I have to find a repairman in German? Oh God, I hope they don't have Super Secret Swiss Appliance Repair Society. It could be WEEKS before I can do my laundry.*

Eventually the maintenance man's wife came and explained, since she speaks pretty good English. She must have spoken to her husband and figured out what was going on. She told me to try the machines again because they were probably just off for the lunch hour. Sure enough, the machines worked.

So, if you ever come to Switzerland, remember that you CAN'T make noise during lunch and especially—NO NOISE ON SUNDAY!

MONEY LAUNDERER

Being a stranger in a strange land made ordinary tasks into complicated, difficult ordeals. Buying a car, getting new glasses, and opening a bank account were big adventures—and they almost didn't let me get a bank account at all.

Right before I moved to Europe, the US government started cracking down hard on tax evaders, and they were especially targeting US citizens who had bank accounts in Switzerland. These new reporting requirements meant the US was slapping heavy fines on any bank in Switzerland that didn't comply, and as a result, it was expensive and difficult for Swiss banks to have US clients. A lot of Americans in Switzerland got kicked out by their Swiss banks.

Not knowing any of this, I grabbed my passport and happily approached my local bank to open an account.

I got to the bank, walked up to the teller, and asked to speak with someone who spoke English about opening an account. After waiting a few minutes I was directed to someone's office and offered a seat. I sat down and said, "Hello, my name is Randy and I would like to open an account."

Immediately, the man's face froze. His nostrils flared, as though he was smelling something rotten.

Uh-oh, I thought.

He said, "My name is Andre. Are you an American?"

"Yeees..." I said cautiously.

He looked pained. "I am sorry, but I cannot help you."

"But I live in Switzerland, here in Kreuzlingen."

"Sorry, but we no longer take Americans as clients. It is too much paperwork."

Wait, what? "But I work for a Swiss company!"

The banker smiled thinly. "Sorry, but we have a new policy not to take any Americans. It does not matter if you live and work here. We have closed all the accounts of Americans. Your government has threatened us with huge fines if we even have a typo on your paperwork. You are just not worth it anymore."

Thinking this must be an isolated case, I thanked him for his time and walked down to the next bank in town. Same thing, as soon as they found out I was American, it was "Sorry, but no." It was too much paperwork, one little mistake and they would get huge fines from the US. "It costs too much to do business with Americans now," they told me, "and it's just not worth it."

I went to every bank in town that day and was rejected by all of them. It was really depressing to have so much rejection in one day.

The next day I went directly to SAP's HR.

"I don't know what to do. I can't open a bank account," I told Lara, the lady who did all my employment paperwork.

"Why not?" she asked, glancing up from her laptop. "Is the language an issue?"

"*No,*" I protested. "They *literally won't let me* open a bank account."

She smiled tolerantly, as though I'd just told her a knock-knock joke. *Cute, but kind of dumb.*

I pressed on. "Can you send me a check instead of doing direct deposit?"

Lara shook her head firmly. "No, it is mandatory that all payroll goes through direct deposit."

"But they won't give me an account!" I repeated, getting frustrated.

She frowned. "What bank did you try"?

When I told her, she looked the bank up and called them. I sat there, hands awkwardly folded on my lap, while she launched into an epic German argument. I couldn't understand a word of it, but people were definitely raising their voices.

After a few minutes, she hung up the phone. "This will be more difficult than I thought," she announced, pursing her lips. "Come with me."

We walked down the hall to Jacqueline's office, the VP of Finance. Lara launched into another vehement discussion, and then Jacqueline turned to me. "So, you're having problems getting a bank account?"

I nodded. "Yes."

"Are you ok with having a bank in Tägerwilen?"

"Um, I guess so?"

"Good, come with me."

So we got in her car and drove to a bank in Tägerwilen. Walking in, I knew right away something was different. Jacqueline was immediately greeted by name, and we were led to the offices of a severe-looking blonde woman by the name of Frau Miller. She reminded me of my elementary school principal, Ms. Winch. Sitting in her office, I figured I was going to either get a bank account or detention.

"Hello Frau Miller, this is Randy, our new employee from America and he would like to open an account with you," Jacqueline began.

Frau Miller frowned. *Uh-oh. Detention.* "I am sorry, but we cannot take American clients at this time. Maybe in a few years if our policies change. I'm sure you understand." She smiled, but her eyes looked cold.

Jaqueline smiled at me. "Is it okay with you if we speak in German, Randy?" she asked. I nodded my head yes.

What followed was a brief but extremely intense exchange. If I'm not mistaken, Frau Miller went a little pale. Then she stood up. "Herr Snow, please follow me and I will have someone set you up with a new account," she said. And so, in just about twenty minutes, it was done.

When we were safely outside the building, I asked Jacqueline what she'd said to get me an account.

Jacqueline just winked. "I told them it would be a shame if SAP, which of course is an international, multibillion-dollar company, had to change banks because they were not able to assist us with such a small request".

RHEINSCHWIMMEN

SWIM! SWIM! Harder or you'll never make it. The current is too strong; I'll miss the exit point, and then I'll be swept downstream forever. I'll never find my way back and I'll be lost in the Swiss wilderness and get eaten by wolves. Or get swept over the falls.

I know the Rheinfalls are somewhere around here, but I don't know how far. We did drive for a while to get here. What if they're just around the corner? Crap!

Must push myself harder. Oh my God, I should not have eaten so much for lunch. My muscles are cramping and I'm out of breath. Good Lord this is a strong current.

Everyone else knew. That's why they already started heading over to the side. I should have been paying attention. WHY DIDN'T I PAY ATTENTION? Now I'll be swept downstream to a watery grave.

How the heck fire did I get into this predicament, anyway?

It all started with a group email, to all the people who worked in the Tägerwilen office. I don't remember the exact wording, but it was an invitation to go to something called *Rheinschwimmen*. I looked it up. The *Rhein* is the Rhine. You know, the big river that flows through Germany and along the borders with France and Switzerland. And *Schwimmen* is, yes you guessed it, swimming.

I liked all the people who were going, so I decided *what the heck, another adventure.* It had to be more fun than opening a bank account. All I knew was, I was supposed to bring a bathing suit and a change of clothes.

The day finally arrived and we all met up after work. We travelled for what felt like forever on the highway. Finally, we pulled off onto a side road, traveled down a few dirt paths, and eventually, we stopped.

We were in a large dirt parking lot in the middle of the woods. I couldn't even see the river yet. The forest was a dense, intimidating green curtain that surrounded us. I wonder what stories those ancient trees could tell. Had they seen knights riding out on horseback, swords drawn against invading armies? Or had they seen villagers risking the unknown as they scavenged for food to feed their families?

Then I got distracted, because everybody started taking their clothes off.

There were my colleagues, getting out of their cars and just stripping down, right out in the open. This was a public place with other people around! They just changed out of their work clothes and pulled on their bathing suits, bare butts winking in the sunshine, without a care in the world.

I was not quite that European yet. Luckily, I'd planned ahead. Before I left work, I'd gone into a restroom and put my swimsuit on under my jeans. My colleagues all laughed at me when they saw I was already wearing my suit. They told me I was a "typical American," but I didn't care.

I was so happy to be out with friends, enjoying local experiences. I put my keys in a Ziploc bag as instructed, and tucked them in the pocket of my trunks.

Eventually, we headed down the path to the river. Everyone jumped in and started swimming out into the middle. When I first jumped in I was a little shocked at how cold the water was, but it didn't take long to get used to. I swam out and joined the group. At first my friend Sascha stayed really close to me, making sure I was okay.

"Swimming in the Rhine is different," he explained, paddling smoothly through the icy water. "It's not like those warm, calm lakes you have back in Texas."

Then he said something else, but I wasn't really paying attention, since I was too busy telling him what a great swimmer I was. After all, I didn't want him to think a Texan couldn't keep up.

There was a bit of a current in the middle of the river, and we let the water carry us along. We drifted downstream, chatting and watching the scenery go by. *I think I'm going to like this Rheinschwimme,* I thought to myself. I was lost in my own world. I lay on my back for a while and watched the clouds, imagining myself floating on their feathery wings. Then I turned over and peered at the trees, hoping to catch a glimpse of a wolf—or maybe a dragon! After all, those thick stands of trees looked like fairy tale land. Anything was possible.

Then I glanced up and noticed everyone was gone. They were fifty feet away from me, swimming for the shore. *What's going on?*

The next thing I knew, one of my friends started shouting at me. "Come on! We're approaching the exit point! We need to get out!"

"What exit point?" I hollered back. *Doesn't this river run all the way to the North Sea?*

But my friend started motioning wildly downstream, where a big red flag was posted. "At the flag!" he yelled. "We need to get out at the flag!"

Well that's no problem, I thought to myself. *I can make it over to that flag in a hot second.*

I was wrong. I started swimming, but I didn't go anywhere. A bend in the river was coming up fast now, and I was about to get pushed around the corner and out of sight.

That's how I ended up in this mess. I gave it everything I had, swimming with all my strength, just to keep up. I almost gave up.

I'm so tired, but I can't quit.

NO.

I need to represent Texas better than this!

So I gave myself a mental kick in the butt and doubled down. I was in a full sprint. Kicking as hard as I could, I told myself, *pull...pull...pull...*with each stroke, I reached out for the water and pushed it behind me. Every stroke was a fight. Me versus the river.

I'm so out of breath. With every stroke, I was gasping for air. I was so focused on swimming as hard as I could, I stopped paying attention to where I was in the water. Finally, I looked up to see how much further I needed to go...and I saw people walking.

I stopped swimming and put my leg down. *I can stand!*

My first thought was, *I made it! I'm not going to die!*

My second thought was, *how long have I been trying to swim in three feet of water?*

Still out of breath, I waded to shore. Everyone dried off and put on the spare clothes they'd stashed there in advance. Next to the parking lot was a Biergarten—our reward for surviving the swim and not going over the falls.

Drinks were ordered and we all sat down to relax. After a few drinks, we ordered dinner. I had a bratwurst and a giant pretzel. We sat outside and enjoyed the evening, with the peaceful sound of the Rhine rushing by, mixed with the joyful sounds of people laughing at me.

"Honestly?" I told them. "I didn't think I was gonna make it. Were we really headed for the falls?"

"No," Sascha dismissed my fears. "The falls are still far away. But you could have got lost in the woods," he warned.

"Is that dangerous? Like are there dragons and stuff?"

He shrugged his shoulders. "No dragons. Just wolves. Also boars. And the occasional brown bear. But dragons—" He smiled wickedly. "I haven't seen one of those things in years."

COWBOY

Everywhere we went, Cowboy was a fan favorite. Swiss people loved his different-colored eyes, they loved that he was called "Cowboy," and they were fascinated that he came over from Texas with me.

My apartment was about a two-minute walk from a convenience store and Cowboy and I would usually stop there on the way back from one of our walks and pick up a few things. Everyone who worked there was so nice. Several spoke English and they would always try to talk to me a little bit and make me feel comfortable. Those who didn't speak English were so patient. One lady was especially nice to me and Cowboy. Maria was the manager at the store. She was about my age and lived with her family nearby. Her English was great, and she always talked to me and made sure I was doing okay. She would tell me about all the upcoming festivals, and the local attractions she thought I might enjoy.

As to Cowboy, he was in LOVE with Maria. Every time we passed by, she'd bring out a hotdog and feed it to him. I would be inside shopping and she'd go outside and find Cowboy to feed him a hotdog and give him a pet. If I was in a hurry and couldn't stop to talk, she'd run out and hand me a hotdog wrapped in a paper towel for me to give Cowboy later. It got to the point where if we walked near the train station, Cowboy would strain on his leash, trying to go in and say hello.

Everywhere we went, people wanted to stop and pet my dog. Lots of people wanted to take a picture with him. But sometimes, all their attention got a little more complicated. One time, my friend Julian and I went out to get some food for a hike, and that was one of the few places where Cowboy wasn't allowed inside. I waited outside with my buddy while Julian went in. I was wearing old clothes and shoes with holes in them, my typical outfit for a long walk in the woods. I got Cowboy some water and sat down on the curb. After a few minutes, an older gentleman with a cane came up to me and started talking.

"Vould you like one of my pretzels?" he asked, with a slightly creepy smile.

"Uh, *nein danke*," I answered. *Why is this guy trying to feed me?*

"Vould you like one of my sausages?" he persisted. "Or perhaps for your little doggy?"

Is he coming on to me? "Sure," I said. *Or maybe he has a thing for Cowboy?* "Thanks."

That guy went away, but people kept coming up to us and offering food. A little while later, a young girl with her mom stopped. She looked at me and pointed at Cowboy, then asked me something in German.

I was pretty sure she wanted to know Cowboy's name, but I was already freaked out by the old guy and didn't feel like talking, so I played the American card.

I shrugged my shoulders. "I'm sorry, but I don't speak German."

Of course she spoke perfect English, so she repeated her question in English. "What is the name of your dog?" she asked, her blue eyes wide and innocent. *Crap, I guess I won't get out of this that easy.*

"This is Cowboy," I told her.

"Can I pet him?"

"Of course, he's very friendly."

She reached down and stroked his head. Then she asked, "I have some extra dog treats—can I give some to Cowboy?"

I couldn't say no. For one thing, it would be rude. For another, it would be a rip-off for Cowboy. "Yes," I said, "thank you."

Then her mom did something completely unexpected and handed her daughter a sandwich. The girl turned to me. "Would you like a sandwich?" she asked. "We have an extra one."

Man, Switzerland sure is a super-friendly place for foreigners. "No, thank you," I said with a smile.

She fed Cowboy a few more treats, while exchanging pleasantries in her perfect, little girl English. As her mother tugged her away, she asked me if I was *sure* I didn't want a sandwich.

Come on Julian, hurry up and finish shopping, this is getting weird out here.

Once the girl and her mother left, I sat there on the curb, petting Cowboy. He had a big grin on his face from all the treats he was getting. After a minute or two, a third person stopped and asked if we wanted food. I politely said no.

Then I looked down at my shoes. They had holes in them. I looked at my hiking shorts. *Stains, not in the best shape.* My shirt had a coffee spill on it.

Then it hit me.

Oh my God. They think I'm homeless!

It was nice that people were offering to help, but that didn't feel right. I decided get up off the sidewalk and take Cowboy on a stroll around the block.

For a homeless guy, I did a lot of fun things with my co-workers. We checked out Oktoberfest and Fastnacht, which is like the German version of Mardi Gras. One day, we did something they called *Wein Wonderung*, where we hiked to a winery. My friends did wine tastings and bought several bottles while Cowboy and I walked around. Then we hiked to a spot on a hill overlooking the lake, where we had a picnic dinner with sandwiches and the wine we just bought. I don't drink myself, so I had a ham sandwich and a Coke. For Cowboy I brought enough food to last a week. We had small treats, large treats, treats to chomp quickly, and special little chewies made from pig ears which he loved.

Soon the sun began to set. As it sank into the water it turned from yellow to orange, as if the water from the lake was putting out the flame. The sky lit up in a rainbow of colors with the clouds reflecting the last of the rays as the sun sank out of sight. Then the stars came out, bright and twinkling. One person even had an app to track satellites, and he pointed them out as they glided past.

That picnic was a good one. But things didn't always go smoothly on walks. One time Cowboy and I were asked to join a couple of friends with their dogs on a walk near Gottlieben , and afterwards, we all planned to have a drink at the lake. We met up at the walking path, and once we were outside town, we all let our dogs off their leashes to run around. It was all going well. They were asking lots of questions about how I was assimilating into Swiss life, and they laughed about my picture-hanging crimes on Sunday.

This part of the countryside was all farm fields, with a few trees scattered along the lake. During the growing season we didn't let our dogs run loose, but when the fields were fallow, nobody minded. We strolled along a path through the pastures, enjoying the sunshine.

We were just about at the halfway point when Cowboy decided to take off. All the other dogs were running around, so at first this didn't concern me—but then I sensed something was wrong. Cowboy looked back at me, and I could see the devil in his eyes. He was about to do something he knew I wouldn't approve of. I hollered at him, but he ignored me and started running.

Oh no, I thought. *What now.* I started running to catch him, hoping to head off his crime before he did something stupid. But it was too late.

Before I could stop him, Cowboy found a great big pile of fresh, stinking cow poop and did a swan dive right into the middle of it. Then he rolled around, making sure it coated every inch of his body.

I could have died of embarrassment right there.

Cowboy was acting all proud like he'd accomplished something great by rolling around in all that poop, but even the other dogs were avoiding him. As for me, I was *pissed*. Not only did I have to walk back home in shame, towing my stinky American poop dog, but now Cowboy needed a bath. And I was going to miss our drinks date at that lovely restaurant we'd chosen, down by the lake.

TEST TIME

Growing up in Texas, I did quite a bit of fishing from an early age. Camping and fishing were just part of the summer experience when I was a kid. Now that I was living in this beautiful country full of pristine lakes and rivers, I figured it was an ideal opportunity to expand my fishing skills. Fishing would be a great excuse for me and Cowboy to get out together on the weekends. We could hike out to a nice remote spot, he could run around or take a nap, and I would catch us our dinner. How cool would that be to eat some fresh Swiss fish I'd caught myself!

All I needed was a license. And how hard can that be? I mean in Texas, I could walk into a sporting goods store, pay a little money, and they handed me a permit.

As usual, I was wrong again. This is Switzerland. Home of wonderful cheese, tasty chocolate, the magnificent Alps, and a universe of complicated regulations.

Getting a fishing license in Switzerland was crazy. It is way worse than applying for my driver's license back in the States. If you want to fish legally in Switzerland, you actually have to take a class and pass an exam. That earns you a general license which allows you to then go to a local store, pay money, and get a region-specific permit.

Just the thought of it made me tired. But I wanted to be able to fish, and I had a friend at work who wanted a fishing license as well, so I asked if we could do it together.

Patrick helped me get enrolled in the course, and he ordered my book for me. When I saw I had a package delivered and it was my fishing book, I got all excited. I thought it would be like a little pamphlet with a few diagrams and some catchy slogans about making sure to be respectful of the other people around you. It was not a pamphlet. It was a freaking big-ass text book. In German.

My heart sank. I thought I'd be able to memorize a few names with a few pictures, and just fake my way through the test. *Nope.* Patrick explained that we had to learn not only how to identify of all the different fish in the country, but where in Switzerland each of them could be found. We would also have to learn the different types of fishing gear you were allowed to use when fishing for each specific kind of fish. Of course you also had to know when you could and could not fish for them, when the different cantons had different seasons for different fish, and the different rules for fishing from a boat versus fishing from the bank. They even had special rules for fishing in a lake versus a river, and a third set of rules for ponds and creaks. Different baits were permitted for different kinds of fish, so that was a whole extended chapter. It was a full-on festival of regulations, and I was supposed to learn it all from reading this German textbook.

Game over man, I am screwed. Oh well, I already made a commitment to go with Patrick and I already paid, so let's just do it for the experience, even if I have no chance in hell of passing.

I knew the textbook wouldn't be much help. But then things got worse. When we went to take the class, it turned out to be all in Swiss German. That's like an American trying to understand a heavy Cockney accent.

I tried to study. Mostly, I looked at the pictures of different Swiss fish and tried to remember a few keywords. I figured that even if I didn't know what the words meant, I could pick the multiple-choice answer that had those words in it.

During class, I just sat there and smiled like an idiot the whole time, pretending to understand what the instructor was saying. When everyone else laughed, I laughed. When everyone looked surprised, I looked surprised. It's amazing how well you can fake it.

Once we finished class, it was time for the final. The instructor passed out the test and I stared at it like it was written in a foreign language. Which it definitely was.

I have no chance of passing this.

Just as I was about to start randomly circling answers, the teacher said something incomprehensible and the room responded with excitement. "What's going on?" I nudged Patrick.

"He says we can do our final in groups and we can help each other at the table."

I went limp with relief. Patrick helped me, all right. I copied every single answer off his paper.

I got a 100 on my exam. And with that, I earned my very own genuine Swiss fishing license.

BLACK FOREST

Cowboy is probably one of the most well-traveled dogs in all of Texas. He's been to Switzerland, Germany, Austria, Italy, France, Spain, Andorra, Monaco, Liechtenstein, Luxembourg, Hungary, Slovakia, Poland, and the Czech Republic. He went everywhere with me when I got time off, and I always made sure we both had a good time. For every day in a city, we would get a day in the country, full of long walks and interesting smells.

Cowboy's spot in the front seat of my car was more like a throne than a car seat. I filled the floor with pillows until they were even with the seat, and then I put a large dog bed on top of that. Finally, I strapped his harness to the seatbelt for safety. He was near enough that I could drive with one hand and pet him with the other. Half the car was filled with my clothes and hiking gear, and the other half was filled with treats, food, and toys for my buddy.

One winter, I found a place for us to visit in the Black Forest, near the border of France and Germany. It was high in the mountains, deep in the woods, and at the edge of developed land. Of course, at that time of year, the mountains were covered in snow. Maybe it wasn't the best time to plan a hike, but Cowboy and I needed some fresh air and adventure.

We arrived Friday night, around 7:00 p.m., then we checked in and unpacked our stuff. The big hike would be in the morning, but we decided to take a little walk before bed. We walked up the dirt road toward the mountain, and I let Cowboy off the leash so he could stretch his legs. After about 40 minutes I was ready to turn around, but then I heard something moving in the woods. Just a faint twig snap with the sound of snow crunching and bushes rustling. Nothing too big or loud, but I guess it was loud enough, because unfortunately Cowboy heard it, too. He took off running.

I tried to catch him, but the brush was too thick and I couldn't keep up. I walked back to the road and started calling him, but I wasn't worried. Every so often, Cowboy would catch a scent and his instincts would kick in. The chase would be all he could focus on. He'd usually be gone for 20 to 30 minutes, then he'd back on his own.

I walked up and down the dirt road, occasionally calling out to him. After about 30 minutes I started to get frustrated because I was tired, cold, and I wanted to get back to our room.

"Come on, Cowboy!" I yelled out. "Get your stupid butt back here!"

A half hour later I started getting scared. *What happened to my buddy? Maybe he circled around and went back to the room?*

I walked back. Just before arriving at our B&B, I ran into the owners, Peter and Claudia, who were out walking their dog. I explained that Cowboy had run off. Had they seen him?

No.

That's when I started praying. *Please Lord, bring my buddy home.*

It was only about ten at night. *I can find him and still get a decent night's sleep.* I went inside, got a drink of water, put on some extra clothes, and headed back out. I traced my steps back to the point where he went off trail. I figured I should be able to track him in the snow, but as it turns out, I'm no Davy Crockett. I found a lot of animal tracks, but I couldn't tell which ones were Cowboy's. Even when I thought I'd found Cowboy's tracks, after a while they just ended.

As the night wore on, my desperation increased. My prayers became more desperate as well. I tried to bargain with God and make promises. *Bring my buddy safely home, God, and I promise I'll go to church again.* After several hours of desperate searching, I decided to go back to base again, praying that Cowboy would be at the doorstep, waiting on me.

He wasn't.

I was out almost three hours looking for him, and I took a little comfort in the idea that if Cowboy had gone down the mountain, he would have found some houses. Twice he'd run off for periods that extended overnight. Both times, the only reason he hadn't come home was that someone had taken him into their home. *Please Lord, let him be warm inside someone's house.*

By that point it was nearing 2 a.m., and of course I couldn't sleep. After warming up a little, I got dressed again and headed back out. 3 a.m., *nothing.* 4 a.m., *nothing.* I spent most of the night patrolling the spot where he'd disappeared, calling for him, retreating to the room to warm up, and going back out again. I cannot describe how scared I was and how terrible I felt. *My buddy's out there, alone. Maybe he's trapped somewhere, waiting for me to come help him.*

Once the sun came up, I took a shower and went to talk to Peter and Claudia. They were concerned too, and they called around to the neighbors, the forest rangers, even the police, asking if anyone had found him. No luck. At that point, I had to trust that God had taken care of my buddy, and he was safely in someone's home. Surely, the police would have been notified of a found dog and I'd be able to go pick him up. *I prayed all night. I made so many promises. Why isn't God answering my prayers?*

Peter was great and helped me tremendously, but he was also a little too blunt.

"I'm sorry to tell you," Peter said, "your dog is most likely dead. There is no one in the forest at this time of year, and the snow is very wet. He will freeze to death and no one will find him." Claudia looked at him with a shocked expression, but I noticed she didn't disagree.

I just shook my head. *No way. My buddy's out there in the cold somewhere and I'm gonna find him.* I packed provisions for a day, bundled up, and headed out into the mountains.

There I was, trudging through the snow, calling out until I was hoarse. The thoughts I had going through my head were not good. I had tears in my eyes. I couldn't stop thinking about Cowboy stuck in the snow, hurt and crying out for me. *Does he think I abandoned him?*

Please God, don't let it end this way – not like this. I'd always understood he would die someday, but I couldn't bear never knowing what happened to him. It broke my heart to think he might be alive, waiting on me to bring him home.

After a while, I started to lose hope. My prayers changed. *Please Lord, help me find his body. Let me find him so I know what happened.* I was already planning how I'd spend the next weekend searching for him. I would never get over this. I would spend every weekend and vacation for the next several years looking for him, if I had to. The idea of him thinking I abandoned him was almost too painful to bear.

But even if I spent years looking for him, I knew the odds were against me. Tears streaming down my face, I realized I was probably never going to see my buddy again. At that point, I couldn't stand anymore and I fell to my knees. I had to accept that he was gone and I needed to figure out how I would deal with it.

As hard as it was, anger and fear would not bring me peace, so my prayers changed again. "God, I need you now more than ever before. I know that I cannot deal with the loss of my buddy, so the only way I will make it through this is if you do it with me."

I stood up and wiped my eyes. I did not know what I would do come Monday, but for this weekend I knew I had to keep looking.

At that moment, my phone rang. I could barely understand the person on the other line. My reception was terrible and whoever it was didn't speak very good English. All I could get from the call was something about "your dog, found, okay."

That was enough. I sprinted down that mountain like an athlete. It took me an hour to get back to the B&B. My heart was racing as I looked everywhere for Cowboy, but I didn't see him anywhere. I knew the reception had been bad, but I didn't think I'd misheard. I was *sure* the guy had said "dog" and "okay."

Finally, I found Peter, and he handed me a piece of paper with an address on it. "Zees is the place," he pointed. "I think Cowboy is there."

I got into my car right away. You cannot imagine how difficult it was to only speed a little. My GPS couldn't find the exact location, but it brought me close. I parked my car and started walking. Finally, I found the house. I walked up to the door and rang the bell, heart hammering in my chest. *What if it's not Cowboy, but some other dog? Please let it be my buddy.*

A young man by the name of Hans answered the door. I saw two dogs in the background, but no Cowboy. The man said something in German.

"Lost dog?" I stammered. "Found dog?"

At that moment, Cowboy turned the corner. I almost knocked the poor guy over as I ran past him into the house. Cowboy was so excited to see me I couldn't even pet him. He'd jump up on me, and before I could grab him he'd take off and run around the couch. He'd jump up on me again, and then run around the kitchen table. He continued to jump up and zoom around for several minutes. Hans's dogs were looking at him like he was some kind of crazy American. When he finally settled down I gave him a great big belly rub and checked him out to make sure he was okay. Thankfully, everything was fine.

Hans switched to English. "I found him ziss morning, when I was walking my dogs. Actually," he chuckled, "it was my dogs that found him. And you know what? It is strange. I don't usually go walking there. But this morning, I just felt like walking in that place in the forest."

Thank you Lord. I knew you were watching out for my buddy.

"Other than being hungry, he seems just fine." Hans laughed. "He ate three bowls of doggy food!"

I was so grateful this guy took the trouble to bring Cowboy home and call the authorities. He could have said it wasn't his responsibility and left Cowboy out there. "Can I pay you?" I asked. "Can I give you money for everything you've done?"

But he just shook his head. "*Nein.* I am happy to help. Cowboy is a tough dog!"

After I got home, I sent Hans's dogs a giant care package full of treats and toys. I think I bought out the whole pet store. "I'll take one of those," I told the shopkeeper, "and three of those, and throw in a handful of those while you're at it." Everything from soft toys, to mini-treats, to big, long-lasting chews. Stuffed toys, rope toys, squeaky toys. Then I wrote a note to Hans:

Dear Hans,

I cannot thank you enough for saving my best friend's life. I know you didn't want a reward, so I am sending this box of gifts for your dogs. The Starbucks gift card is for your dogs, too. But they can share it with you if they feel like it.

Your friend,

Randy

Everyone was amazed that my city dog made it through the night in the frozen, remote mountains of the Black Forest. I mean this is the same place where the Grimm brothers found inspiration for their creepy fairy tales. It's basically the same woods where Hansel and Gretel were kidnapped by a witch. These are not the woods that mere mortals should trifle with. So the Swiss folks were amazed by my buddy, but not me. After all, he's a Texan. Plus, his name is Cowboy.

BODENSEE BLUES

I lived on this incredibly beautiful lake called Lake Constance, or *Bodensee*, as they call it in German. It's the largest lake in Germany, and it's so big that it borders three countries: Switzerland, Germany, and Austria. When I first moved here, everyone told me I should plan a bike trip around the lake. It sounded like a fantastic idea.

The only problem was my buddy. Cowboy can't ride a bike, and I didn't think he'd enjoy being pulled along in a trailer. He likes to walk around and sniff things.

Wait, that's it! We can walk around the lake and sniff things. Brilliant idea.

Okay, actually I'm not that into sniffing things. I'll leave the sniffing to Cowboy and I'll focus more on the walking. All I need is a backpack and I'll be good to go!

Easier said than done.

THE PACKING
One backpack, that's all I get? One tiny little bag?

Yes, I went to a sporting goods store. Yes, I talked to the experts. Yes, I bought the expensive big trekking backpack that was recommended. At the time it looked humongous, but apparently it shrank. Now that I need to fit everything in, it's tiny. One tiny little bag.

So here I am. One big pile of stuff and one tiny little bag. *I'm never going to fit everything in. I need to start prioritizing.*

Okay, food for Cowboy, check.
Treats for Cowboy, check.
Toys for Cowboy, check.
Water bowl and extra water for Cowboy, check. I know we're walking around a lake and shouldn't need extra water, but what if something happens and we get stranded somewhere and can't get to the lake? Gotta make sure Cowboy's okay.

Now that all the important stuff is packed, how much room do I have left over for my stuff?

Very little. Okay, I'm not going to be able to take all my hiking clothes. Do I really need more than one shirt?

I pack in as much stuff as I can fit, and then I'm ready to go.

THE PLAN

The plan is simple. Start walking, and stop for the night when we get tired. Wake up and repeat. We have only two rules. The first rule is that we need to stay as close to the water's edge as possible, even if it means not staying on the path. The second rule is to have no other rules. If we feel like walking, we walk. If we want to stop and sniff around, we stop. We do not reserve hotels in advance. We go where we want, and we stay where we want. We are free.

Looking back, I wish we'd had more rules.

THE PROSTITUTE

We wake up and it's a beautiful day! A great day to begin an adventure. I take a quick shower, down a cup of coffee, and I'm ready to go. I double-check to make sure I have everything. I start to put my backpack on. This tiny little backpack is not so tiny. Actually it's pretty heavy and bulky. I manage to strap it on, and then I start to get Cowboy ready. Bad idea. I stagger around and practically fall over. Next, I take my backpack off and put the harness on Cowboy. Then I put my backpack back on. It is now midmorning. We are off.

We walk to the water's edge and turn left, toward Tägerwilen. We are in high spirits. Cowboy is enjoying the walk. He is stopping and sniffing and occasional peeing to tell all his dog buddies where he's been.

Staying close to the water takes us to Konstanz, and now we're in Germany. It's amazing, really—something you just don't think about as an American. In ten minutes, we go from Switzerland to Germany. In about 20 minutes we'll be back in Switzerland. As a Texan, it's hard to comprehend how many countries you're close to when you're in Switzerland. In Texas I can drive for eight hours and still be in Texas. Meanwhile, here I am about to WALK around a lake that takes me through three countries. If I drive for eight hours, depending on my direction I could make it to France, Italy, Austria, Hungary, the Czech Republic, Slovenia, or the Netherlands. I'm guessing that's why they speak so many languages out here.

We follow the water until we get to the Imperia Statue. The Imperia is a statue of a giant prostitute that is holding a king in one hand and a pope in the other. That's also the kind of thing we don't see so much in Texas.

THE RULES

We follow the lake until we leave Germany and cross back into Switzerland, and the trail just keeps getting more beautiful. Beech and oak trees keep us shaded under an overhead canopy. They're thick enough to make us feel like we're alone in a deep forest, but there's still plenty of room for Cowboy to scamper down to the water and take little swims to cool off and get a drink. Every now and then Cowboy runs ahead, darting left and right to make sure his nose doesn't miss anything. I feel kind of bad for all the flowers he pees on, especially those periwinkle blue forget-me-nots. This path is a rainbow of colors and a smorgasbord of smells. *Life is good.*

As we approach Gottlieben, I put Cowboy back on the leash. This is the village where we lived when we first came to Switzerland, the place where I survived on bread and water because I couldn't find food, the place where I almost died because I couldn't ask for medicine. I can see the church bells that caused me to tear around hunting for a fire. It all seems so quaint now.

In the afternoon, we find a nice restaurant with seating outside in a garden. Cowboy and I decide it's a good place to stop for lunch. Hiking in Europe can be very civilized if you want it to be. In Switzerland, they even have something called a *Waldschenke.* Essentially, it's a seasonal restaurant out in the forest, open just for the summer. You can only get to it by hiking or biking, which is handy when you want fresh food or a terrific cup of coffee in the wilderness.

We find a shady table with a good view of the lake. I pour Cowboy a bowl of water and then order a classic Rhineland dish called *Käsespätzle.* It sounds exotic, but basically it's a heavenly version of mac and cheese. When my food comes, I give Cowboy a bully stick to chew on so we can eat together. Then I have a cup of coffee while Cowboy rests and finishes his meal.

After the coffee, we keep walking towards Stein Am Rhein. At first we feel pretty good, but after a few hours of the sun beating down on us, we're both getting tired. I'm also getting frustrated. My "stay near the lake" rule means we sometimes veer off the path and the trail disappears completely. Then we have to backtrack, so we lose a couple of hours wandering around in circles. The "stay near the lake" rule is starting to look like a very dumb rule.

The other rule—my "no rules" rule—I end up breaking completely. We pass several nice hotels, but I'm fixated on getting to Stein Am Rhein the first day. I don't know why. I guess I feel like we haven't walked enough. If I stop too soon, I'll be a wimp. It doesn't matter that this is our first day and we haven't adjusted to this type of hiking yet, or that we've already passed through TWO different countries in the past five hours. No, I would be a wimp to stop.

This is stupid.

We keep walking and walking. My tiny little backpack is starting to feel huge. Not only that, but our road has veered away from the lake so we can't go for a swim to cool down. I'm hot, I'm tired, and my feet hurt.

I decide it's time to stop. I start looking for a hotel. Unfortunately, we're in a stretch along the lake with no towns. There's nowhere to stop. I find a small bush with enough shade for Cowboy and we take a break. I pour him some more water and he has a little rest.

The we start walking again. I heft the giant backpack and put it on my back. *Good Lord this thing weighs a ton.* I adjust the behemoth, and we start trudging forward. *You stupid dumb-ass, why didn't you stop when you had a chance? You knew you were getting tired, but no, you had to prove you could go longer. Dumb-ass. What the hell did you pack in this mega-size backpack and why did you need to buy such a huge one? Good God man, you could fit an elephant in this thing, and it feels like you did.*

We have no choice but to keep going.

THE RESCUE

By the time we approach a hotel, I must look like a professional bum. I'm sweaty, I stink, and every part of my exposed skin is burned bright red. I'm limping from the blisters on my feet, and Cowboy looks like a wild lake dog. He's been in and out of the water all day.

The hotel, on the other hand, is fancy. It's located at a winery and they have their own grapes growing on the property. It will be expensive. I do not care. I walk up to the entrance, trudge inside, and ask for a room.

The lady behind the desk glances at me and makes a quick assessment. "This is not a budget hotel," she informs me. "Rooms start at €200." I can understand her concern. She looks like a librarian with her hair in a bun, glasses at the edge of her nose, golden chain clipped on them so they will not fall off and get lost. She is impeccably dressed in a long skirt and heels. It's clear she's used to a different type of guest.

I do not care. I am done.

She sniffs. "Ze dog cannot stay in ze main hotel. But zer are rooms at ze back."

"That's fine," I nod.

"Zey are not as nice," she warns.

"No problem."

"But zey cost ze same."

Her smile looks triumphant, but she can't scare me off that easy. I do not care. The house I am carrying on my back needs to come off. She checks us in and takes us to our room.

I've never been so happy to see a bed in my life. Cowboy and I crawl under the sheets and fall fast asleep.

THE WALKING DEAD

The next day we make it to Stein Am Rhein with no problems. From here it's not long before we cross into Germany again. Yesterday we were dying in the sun and today it's pouring rain. This wouldn't be a big deal, except now an enormous blister is forming on my foot.

I stop at an Apotheke to buy some Band-Aids. The pharmacist sells me a box of something, but they don't look like Band-Aids. However, I'm a seasoned traveler by now. I figure these are German Band-Aids. I stick one on my foot.

That night when I'm getting undressed, I peel it off like a normal Band-Aid.

This is a BAD IDEA.

It is not a normal Band-Aid. It's some kind of fake German skin that's melded with my skin. When I rip it off, it takes off the blister and all the surrounding skin and flesh. Where I once had a foot, I now have a raw chunk of meat. The pain is excruciating. I almost can't walk.

Luckily, I have decided to stick to Rule #2: There Are No Rules. For the rest of the trip, when we get tired, Cowboy and I start looking for a hotel. Now that I have half my foot missing, that's a welcome relief.

FANCY PANTS

On the last day of our trip, Cowboy and I stumble across a luxury resort that's right on the water. It looks like a great place to end our lake adventure in style. By the time we get there, we're both filthy and exhausted. I'm limping from my injured foot, and Cowboy looks like a beast.

Fancy cars are pulling up to the resort entrance, with all of these really glamorous people getting out. One valet takes their luggage, while another valet parks their cars. I'm a bum with a dog and a raggedy backpack. I'm expecting them to turn us away.

A valet starts walking toward me. *Here we go.*

"Guten Tag," he says with a smile. *"Kann ich deinen Rucksack für dich nehmen?"*

Wait a minute. Did he just offer to take my backpack for me?

"Nein danke," I reply. He then smiles and tells me to have a nice day.

I shake my head. *Okay, he was cool, but what's going to happen when I try to get into the lobby?*

I enter the building and limp up to the counter. With a wet thud, I drop my monster backpack to the ground. Cowboy lies down on the tiles, still damp and muddy from an earlier swim. "Excuse me," I ask warily. "Do you speak English?"

The young lady behind the counter looks up. She's wearing a turquoise silk scarf knotted at the neck, and her shiny brown hair is pulled back in a gold clip. "Of course," she replies with a smile. "Would you like a room for you and your dog?"

"Um, yes please," I stammer, expecting to be directed to the servant's quarters out back. *Or maybe a stable? The way we look, I'd put us in a stable right now.*

Wrong again.

"We have several suites available," she offers, "as well as double rooms and single rooms."

I get a double room. When I can afford it, I always get the double room. They usually come with a king-size bed, which is handy when you're sharing with a mud-covered lake dog. This one's expensive, but we deserve it.

We spend the rest of the afternoon relaxing by the lake, me sipping coffees and fruit drinks, Cowboy chewing on bully sticks, dog biscuits, and chicken jerky. Treats and a sunset: the perfect ending to our adventure.

But we're both done walking for awhile. The next morning, we take a boat across the lake to Rorschach Switzerland and from there, we take a train home.

NEWBIE

Have you ever tried a new experience, only to find that you're completely out of your depth? You think you're doing just fine, until you jump into a situation that demonstrates exactly what a total newbie you are.

When that happens, your only choice is to keep pushing through. If you make it, it'll be "a learning experience." If not, well—you don't make it.

I've had that happen to me a few times. One was my motorcycle trip from Dallas to San Diego. That was the trip when I learned how to ride a motorcycle. I *thought* I knew what I was doing because I could ride around town or to work and back. Nope. *You* try getting out on the road for three days straight. Naturally you have a sore butt, but that's just the start of your problems. How about squeezing a throttle for eight hours straight? Now I know there's a little spin wheel to keep the throttle in place, but I didn't figure it out till my hand cramped up like a claw. That was a learning experience.

Another one was my hike up into the Swiss Alps. And that time, I almost didn't make it.

Hey, I walked around Lake Constance. That makes me a hiker, right?

Nope.

I knew nothing, NOTHING!

It seemed pretty straightforward at the time. Cowboy and I joined a hiking club that was located in the city of Saint Gallen, right at the edge of the Alps. Their next outing was described as a moderate hike that would take three hours. *Perfect, we'll be home for lunch.*

I should have known better.

On the day of the hike, I grabbed my day pack. It had a Camelbak for water, and it was just big enough for a couple of extra water bottles, some treats for Cowboy, and a sandwich for me.

The weather looked great, fine and sunny with a cloudless blue sky. I packed light, figuring I could just buy a sandwich at the meeting spot. But when we got there, I couldn't find the other hikers—and when I finally found them, there wasn't a store in sight. *Whoops.*

First lesson: pack what you need before you leave.

I opened my car to pull out my backpack, and that's when I noticed a wet spot on the seat. It turned out that I'd laid my backpack down on the drinking valve of the Camelbak, and half my drinking water had spilled out. But I wasn't too worried; I'd been hiking before and I'd never had water issues in the past.

Big mistake. Huge.

Cowboy and I walked over to meet the two other hikers. One was a slightly older gentleman who looked like he'd hiked across Europe multiple times. He was tall and lean, with long legs for taking long strides. His name was Elias. He had a beard and a mustache and reminded me more of a rugged American outdoorsman than a typical European. The other member of the party was a younger woman. She didn't look as seasoned as Elias, but she was young, healthy and fit. Her name was Clair. Both immediately came up to us and introduced themselves.

"Does your map include topographical notations?" Elias wanted to know.

"My...what?" I said, suddenly feeling unprepared. "I don't have a map. I think I thought it was gonna be signposted and stuff."

Clair looked shocked, but Elias smiled widely. He clapped me on the back. "Don't worry!" he said. "I have a very good map. Plus, I have done this trail many times before."

The hike started off very pleasantly, with the three of us talking and getting to know each other. The scenery was outstanding. Despite clouds in the distance, it was a sunny day. Out here in the middle of the Swiss Alps, the air was crisp and invigorating. The mountains all around us looked like they were reaching out to touch the sky. We were walking along a small stream that wound its way through a meadow carpeted in wildflowers. You could hear cowbells tinkling as happy Swiss cows wandered nearby, enjoying the warm sunshine and eating fresh grass. I think that's the reason why their cheese and chocolate are so good in this country: their milk comes from happy Swiss cows.

Normally when I hike, I am out in the middle of the Black Forest and it's just Cowboy and me. There, I let him off the leash and I walk at a normal pace. He stops and sniffs for awhile as he pleases, then runs and catches up with me. We always make really good time. But on this hike, I had to keep Cowboy on the leash. There were just too many cows and goats around, and I was worried he would take off chasing them.

After an hour or so, I noticed the first sign of trouble.

Cowboy kept stopping to sniff around and enjoy himself, but Elias and Clair wanted to move. I found myself falling behind several times and having to trot to catch up. After about a half hour of this, Elias stopped and gathered us all around.

"I am sorry," he announced, "but this pace is too slow for me. I am going to go on ahead."

Okay, that's cool, I thought. *Only you have the map.*

"Uh, I don't have a map. How will I know what way to go if you leave us?"

Elias' smile froze. "The trail is obvious. Or you can just go back now." Then he turned and walked away.

Clair lowered her head. "I am sorry," she mumbled, then hurried to catch up with Elias.

So there we were, just me and Cowboy. We were low on water, we had no food, and no map. *Oh well,* I thought, *we've been hiking before, we got this.* At least we didn't have any pressure to hurry. *Plus, those guys said it was just a three-hour hike. What problems could we possibly have?*

The answer to that question is: plenty. Plenty of problems.

It took less than ten minutes for Clair and Elias to disappear over a hill, and I never saw them again. Half an hour later, we came across a gang of goats hanging out on the trail, looking like they were up to no good. And those goats had it IN for Cowboy. As soon as they saw us they charged us, putting their heads down and lunging at Cowboy. I kicked and swung my walking pole at them, but they just kept on coming.

Finally, Cowboy had enough. He wiggled out of his harness and bounded over to the goats. And that's when all hell broke loose. I jumped on top of Cowboy, trying to hold him down. I was also shielding him with my body so the goats couldn't headbutt him. I was trying to wrestle his harness back on, but Cowboy kept thrashing and I couldn't hold him down, keep the goats at bay, and get the harness up over his head.

Then I noticed a woman running at us in a pair of muddy overalls, swinging a great big stick. *Great,* I thought. *Just what I need, a beating.*

Thankfully, I was wrong about that, because she started hitting at the goats and pushing them away from Cowboy and me. She kept the goats contained while I shoved the harness back on Cowboy. Then she escorted us out of the area, using her stick to clear us a path. She didn't speak any English, and I was so stressed out and busy with Cowboy I that I couldn't figure out her Swiss German. I never got her name. All I could manage was a *Danke* as we made our escape

Here's another thing I learned that day: I don't like goats.

We tried to stay on the main trail, but at one point we had to cross a large patch of snow and ice. It was very slick, about 30 yards across, and it stretched down the mountain on a steep slope. Gingerly, I set out on the ice. I took it slow, one step at a time. And at first, everything went fine.

Then I slipped.

As I watched my feet fly over my head, I knew this was going to hurt. I came down hard on the ice, dropping the leash so I wouldn't drag Cowboy along with me. Then I started sliding down the ice slick, totally out of control. I tried digging my feet into the snow, but no luck. I tried grabbing at the snow, to no avail. As I picked up speed, all I could do was try to minimize the damage. I did my best to keep my feet crossed in front of me and my arms around my head, trying to protect my face and skull. Eventually, I ran out of snow and crashed into a pile of rocks.

Cowboy had been chasing me, and now he came up beside me and started licking my face, peering at me with wide eyes as if he were really scared I was hurt. I moved slowly at first, making sure I wasn't going to slide anymore, and that nothing was broken.

I got really lucky. Torn clothes, lots of blood, sore muscles, but nothing broken. I was able to walk. I could carry my pack, and nothing had fallen out of it.

I tried to walk back up the ice slick, but that was impossible. Then I saw a small path leading in the right direction, so I followed that, hoping it would join up to the main trail later on. But after another half-hour of walking, the trail disappeared. I looked around and couldn't find it anywhere. All around me, in every direction, all I could see were mountains...and had no idea how to get down.

Cowboy and I were lost in the Swiss Alps, with practically no gear.

Now I could see clouds forming on one of the mountain ridges. I didn't want to get caught out in the open in a storm, so I decided to keep walking and try to find a way back to the main trail. Eventually, I spotted what looked like an abandoned cabin in the distance. I set a new course for the cabin. Even though we still had a lot of daylight, I was playing it safe. At least we'd have shelter. We could spend the night and figure out what to do the next day.

We got to the cabin and I started to walk around it, trying to find the best way to break in. But as I came to the rear of the cabin, the trail started up again! That HAD to be the way back to civilization.

We decided to have a water break. I poured out a little water for Cowboy and that's when I noticed that we didn't have much left. I decided not to drink, and saved it for my buddy instead.

We kept walking and the clouds never rolled in. Up and down, up and down. I felt like those Alps were teasing me. We'd come over a rise and just ahead of us, we'd see a peak. We'd get up there and the path would pitch downwards, so then I'd push myself: *Come on, last peak.* We'd finally get to the top and I would look over...just to see another damned peak in front of me. More hills, more climbing, just to get to the next peak that again was not the peak. It was frustrating and exhausting—but the worst part was, I had no way of knowing if we were even on the correct trail, or how far from civilization we were. As my thirst grew and my throat dried out, I started thinking about all the water I'd dumped on the backseat of my car. Not to mention, this boy from Texas may have been in shape, but I was used to flat prairies. The air up here in the mountains was awfully thin. I was having a hard time breathing.

About five hours into our three-hour hike, I was thirsty, sore, tired, and afraid. I pulled out my cell phone, thinking it might just be time to call for help. *No service.* I gave Cowboy a few more drinks of water, but it wouldn't be long until we ran out completely. My mouth and throat were so dry I could barely talk. All we could do was keep going. My body hurt all over from the fall, from exhaustion, from thirst. Every step was painful.

Trying to motivate myself, I cast my thoughts back to the days when I was a freshman at Texas A&M University. I kept telling myself, "Come on Fish Snow, keep moving!" It sounds ridiculous, but there's a reason for it. As freshmen, they called us "Fish," and of course my last name is Snow. So I'd be out with the Corps of Cadets doing sprints and get to the point where I absolutely could not go on without puking or dying, and Coach Cheney would get up in my face, spit flying out of his mouth, face red, and scream, "Keep moving Fish Snow! Don't you quit on me!"

I wasn't so happy about it at the time, but that day, lost in the mountains, I was glad for Coach Cheney. I knew that even when I thought I was done, I could reach down deep and still find some kind of strength to keep me going.

As the day wore on, I started to worry about nightfall. Peak after peak kept rising up in front of us, and as far as I could tell, there was no end in sight. Finally, getting on towards twilight, we came across a group of other hikers on the trail. I saw them approaching in the distance, and my whole body flooded with relief.

FINALLY, some help! But wait. What if I'm hallucinating and it's just a mirage?

I looked down and Cowboy and he was staring at the hikers, his ears perked up and alert. *Nope, not a mirage.* As they got closer, I could see this group was all decked out in brightly-colored hiking gear, obviously well prepared. There were four of them, two men and two women, their cheeks glowing and flushed with good health and exercise.

Once they were about ten feet away, their eyes got huge as they took in the mess of us. I was covered in dirt and dry blood, my clothes were torn, and I could barely hold my head up.

"How much further until we get to a town?" I managed to gasp, my throat all scratchy and dry.

"Just follow the trail," one of the young girls replied. "Soon you will come to the trailhead with a bus stop."

"Excellent, thanks," I croaked.

She tilted her head in concern. "Are you okay?"

"We're doing much better knowing that we're headed toward a bus stop," I told her.

She pulled a frosty water bottle out of her pack. "Are you sure? Do you need some water?"

Damn, that water looks delicious. I should have said yes, but I can be an idiot. I don't like asking for help. Fish Snow could just power his way to the bus stop.

"No thank you, we're fine," I lied, pulling on Cowboy's leash for us to go.

I waved goodbye and Cowboy and I headed on down the path with dreams of a bus stop dancing in our heads.

After another grueling hour and a half, even Fish Snow was ready to die. And that's when we came to a restaurant at the top of a cable car system. *We're going to make it.* The emotion of knowing the ordeal was over was overwhelming. I wanted to get down on my knees and give Cowboy a hug, but I was worried I wouldn't be able to get up again.

Cowboy had his tail high in the air a spring in his step as we walked into the restaurant. I, on the other hand, was a little more tragic. All I could say was *"Wasser, wasser!"*

The bartender had been having a nice conversation with a pleasant-looking couple at the bar, and he looked up with an angry expression.

Then he saw me.

"Of course, of course, have a seat anywhere. I'll bring water right away."

"Thank you," I groaned. He handed me a large glass of cold mountain spring water and I chugged it down, water pouring down my face and the front of my shirt. It was awesome.

"Are you okay?" he asked.

"YES," I told him, and this time, it was true. "But could I get two more glasses, please? One for me, and one for my dog here."

When the bartender returned with two more glasses, I asked how long it was until the next ride down the mountain.

"One hour," he said. "But it's a very nice hike. You can walk to town in you prefer."

I just laughed. I told him I could wait. I was done with hiking for the day.

INTO THE VOID

You'd think I would have learned not to overestimate my hiking skills, but NOPE.

About the middle of April, we took a trip to a place called Lauterbrunnen. It's a valley in Switzerland that looks like it's right out of a postcard, with a thousand waterfalls pouring out of the surrounding cliffsides. By the time we got there, Cowboy and I were joking about how strong the wind was. The waterfalls were blowing horizontally across the valley, and we both thought that was pretty funny.

Cowboy and I had our own way of communicating. I'd tell him something funny about the wind and laugh, and he'd smile and wag his tail in reply. When I was scared, he'd tuck his tail in and look around nervously. When I was chatting with a friend, he'd look up at me and perk up his ears or prance. Obviously he couldn't talk, but he might as well have been. After living together for so long, I could read his body language and interpret all his funny little facial expressions.

That evening we tucked up into bed, dreaming about the next day's hike we had planned. Little did we know that the wind we'd noticed was the leading edge of a storm that would blast through the mountains and throw us right into a nightmare.

BOOM! A blast of thunder shook the windows, making sure we were wide awake. Next came the wind, howling across the rooftops. It felt like it would blow our hotel off its foundations.

The next morning the damage in town was minimal, but the storm had done a number up in the mountains.

I had just finished breakfast and was sipping on some coffee when the innkeeper came up and started chatting with us.

"Did you sleep all right with the storm last night?" he asked.

"Quite well," I replied. "I needed to get some rest for my hike today."

"Are you walking into the valley? It's very pretty. You can see waterfalls flowing all around there."

I finished my coffee and set down my cup. "No, we're going to head up into the mountains and get in a good hike. I'm hoping we'll get a wonderful view of the valley."

His face went from a smile to a look of concern.

"Better not to hike," he warned us. "The trail can be dangerous, after a storm."

"Huh," I said doubtfully, getting to my feet. "But you think the valley would be ok?"

His smile came back right away. "Yes, yes. A walk in the valley would be fine. That would be best for today."

"Okay," I told him. "A walk in the valley it is, then!"

But what I was really thinking was: *Pshaw. Cowboy and I are from Texas.*

We weren't going to let a storm and a few downed trees stop us, so we loaded our gear and headed up the mountain.

Sure, we had to climb over a few trees that were blocking our path, and at one point it looked like a small avalanche had taken out the trail, but that was no big deal.

Actually, the avalanche was kind of scary. It was on the side of the mountain, and on the other side was a pretty good drop-off.

But we were handling it! We were seasoned hikers!

Eventually, we made it high enough that we hit snow. At first, it wasn't very deep. We even made it to a clearing that had a gondola landing. During the summer, this would be full of people riding the cars up and down the mountain to get a view of the breathtaking scenery. I checked my map, and I was pretty sure I knew which way to go. With the snow on the ground, I couldn't see the trail anymore, but that wasn't a problem. *How hard can it be, right?*

Don't answer that.

We headed further up the mountain in the direction where I thought I would find my next landmark. The snow got deeper and deeper, and eventually it got harder for Cowboy and me to keep moving. At some point, the snow got so deep that Cowboy couldn't walk anymore by himself. I had to stay behind him and push him up over the snowbanks.

I don't know how it happened. One minute we were ankle-deep in snow, the next we were waist-deep and I had no idea where we were. I finally decided it was getting too hard, especially for my short buddy. It was time to turn around. I thought I could just follow our footprints back the way we came, but our footprints had disappeared.

We were lost.

Cowboy started wandering off, but I called him back. That dog can get lost in his own backyard, so I took the lead as we started heading down the mountain. But Cowboy kept trying to go his own way.

"Knock it off, dummy!" I finally snapped at him, frustrated. We had to get back to safety. I'd already lost him once in the Black Forest, and I didn't want to go through that again. Besides, I was the one with the map. I knew which way we had to go.

I kept pushing us in the direction of the hotel, but that fool dog kept trying to yank me another way. I wouldn't listen to him. I knew where to go.

"Come ON, Cowboy!" I hollered. "We don't want to get stuck up here." It's hard work trudging through the snow, even going downhill. This deep in the forest, it was easy to get disoriented. All I could see was trees and snow, trees and snow. I keep pushing branches out of my way and trying to climb over the snowbanks while keeping an eye on my dog to make sure he didn't run off. "This way, Cowboy," I coaxed him, as I pushed a branch out of my face and lifted my boot to take another step.

But this time I didn't see trees OR snow. After moving that branch, all I saw was gray sky. Nothing but air.

I looked down, and my heart leapt in my chest. My foot was stepping off a ledge into the abyss. Slowly, I leaned my body weight back. I brought my foot back to solid ground as I desperately reached for the branch I'd just pushed away. I caught the branch at the last second. I pulled as hard as I could, praying the branch was sturdy and wouldn't break.

Luck was with me that day. I pulled myself back to the safety of the snow.

Cowboy, that clever devil, had stayed back. This whole time, he'd been trying to tell me and I just wouldn't listen. When I was finally safely away from the edge, I sat down and took a breath. According to my estimations, we shouldn't have been anywhere near a cliff. I had no idea where we were or how to get down.

We were in deep snow and in deep trouble.

I turned to Cowboy. "What do you think, Buddy? Do *you* know how to get down?"

He looked at me as if to say that he'd been *trying* to get me to follow him for the past few hours, but I kept yelling at him to come with me.

"Okay, old buddy. When you're right, you're right. You're in charge now. Show me where to go, and I'll follow."

I was so relieved when we made it back to the gondolas and were able to find our path again.

EVA

I met Eva in the summer of 2016, and she's been by my side ever since.

She's pretty shy, and she hates having her picture taken. She's also not real comfortable with me writing about her in this book. Sometimes I tease her about being a spy or in a witness protection because of the effort she goes to not be noticed. But it's hard not to notice a girl like Eva. She's smart, hardworking, adventurous, caring, and beautiful.

Eva speaks four languages: Hungarian, German, English, and Spanish—and she's learning Chinese. She's always on the computer, soaking up more knowledge. She has a bachelor's degree in business, she's a certified dog trainer, and I can't even count how many different teacher certifications she has.

But honestly? It's her golden heart that I find most beautiful about Eva. I tell her she's my golden-hearted angel.

Eva doesn't just care about people and animals, she *acts* on her compassion. When she sees an injured animal, she doesn't just say, "aw, that poor little creature." Nope, she goes and finds a cat carrier or a cardboard box, and she takes the stray to a rescue facility—or else sometimes, she makes me do it.

And then there's Hannes, a homeless man who lives in the park where we walk Cowboy. Eva makes sure I'm always carrying some money in case we see him so we can give it to him. She makes him care packages with everything from essentials like soap and clean socks, to good chocolate and a mystery novel—"Because," she says, "just living is not enough. You have to enjoy yourself, too!"

Did I mention how creative she is? One Christmas a present from Cowboy appeared under the tree. It was a calendar full of pictures of me and Cowboy, and the caption on the cover read, "If I know what love is, it is because of you."

As smart and intellectual as she is, that girl knows how to make me laugh. One evening we were on a walk before bed and it started to rain. I told Cowboy he either needed to do a reverse rain dance, or poop quick so we could get back inside. "Forget the rain dance," Eva told me. "We need to do a poop dance!" Then she started dancing around, chanting "Poop Cowboy, poop! Poop Cowboy, poop!" And the crazy thing is, she could probably have sung that song in Chinese if I'd asked her to.

Eva and I have had some fantastic times together, but the first adventure we shared was a conversation. My German, as I've mentioned, is basic. Eva's English is pretty good, but we've had a few misunderstandings.

One evening, we were out walking Cowboy after dinner. Everything was going fine, and the summer air was gentle and soft. Then all of a sudden, Eva stopped talking.

"What's wrong?" I wanted to know.

"Nothing," she replied, in a tone of voice that told me something was *definitely* wrong.

"Eva, come on," I coaxed. "We were having such a nice talk, and then you went all quiet."

Eva stopped walking and turned toward me. "Why did you call me a jerk?"

I was dumbfounded. "I...I...*when did I call you a jerk?*"

"Just now," she insisted. "When I was holding Cowboy's leash. You told me I was being a jerk."

Suddenly, it dawned on me. It was all I could do not to burst out laughing, but I was afraid she would think I was teasing her. "Eva," I explained. "I told you not to *jerk on the leash.* That means pull it hard, like this." I demonstrated.

"So...you were not saying that I *am* the jerk?"

"Of course not, my angel. I'd never do that."

So we both had a good laugh, and I took her out for gelato.

Then there was the day she fell off her bicycle. I took her to the hospital so we could get an X-ray, but the radiology department was taking awhile. Eventually I couldn't hold it anymore. "Eva," I whispered. "I'm just going to go find a restroom."

Eva looked up, a perplexed look on her face. "But why?"

"Why what?"

"Why would you want to take a nap *now*? Now, when I need to get my hand X-rayed?"

Restroom. Nap room. *Face palm.*

That one was pretty good, but my favorite Eva English moment was when she couldn't remember the word for booger and she called it a "nose poop." That one had me laughing so hard I told some friends at work about it.

Later that day, we were in a serious company meeting when Dominik said, "Excuse me, I have a nose fart," and then he pulled out a tissue and blew his nose.

Being in a bilingual relationship has moments of goofy humor, but Eva's always solid when life gets hard. When my father's cancer took a bad turn, she was there for me. I'd barely hung up the phone with my mother when she told me to go back to the US right away to be with him. She would take care of Cowboy. Because of her, I was able to be there for my dad when he needed me most, and I was able to say goodbye before he died.

That's just love. And it's pretty much the same in any language.

DOVE FARE PIPÌ

One Saturday morning early in May, Cowboy and I caught the train into Venice.

We'd never been to Venice before, so I wasn't sure what to expect. I knew it was underwater, so I half expected the train to drop us off outside of the city and we'd have to find a boat or swim to get there. I was wrong. Turns out, they do have roads, and the train took us right into town.

Of course the first thing I had to check out was the Grand Canal, which was just like a set out of Hollywood. It was full of gondolas, with gondoliers using those long poles to take tourists around the city. But gondolas weren't the only vessels—I saw speed boats, tiny skiffs, kayaks, large passenger boats and even delivery barges taking crates of supplies to the stores and restaurants. And what really took me by surprise were the *colors*. Houses and storefronts were painted lemon yellow, terracotta, and pink, with wooden shutters in bright green and aqua. If you didn't look at the people and just focused on the architecture, you could travel back in time. I liked to imagine Elizabethan courtiers tripping along the narrow streets, taking care not to scuff their silk shoes on the cobblestones.

Cowboy, on the other hand, wasn't impressed. There wasn't much grass in Venice, and that's where he was used to doing his business. There were cobblestones, and Renaissance architecture, and arched bridges over glittering canals, but no grass. We did find one park where Cowboy could relieve himself, and he thought that was pretty excellent, so every few hours we'd venture back to his park. We looked around for some souvenirs, but it wasn't easy to shop with Cowboy—and anyway, I would much rather walk around, or just get a coffee and people-watch. Cowboy loved to stop for coffee because that meant he would get a bowl of water and a continuous supply of treats until we were ready to leave.

And of course, the Italians loved him. *"Che bel ragazzo!"* they'd croon, stopping to pat him on the head. *"Che carino!"* I don't think many people bring their dogs to Venice, so Cowboy must have thought he was world-famous.

Since we couldn't get much shopping done, and Cowboy wasn't a fan of the ancient architecture, we ended up spending a lot of time eating. One of my favorite Venetian dishes was the *Fritto Misto*, which in Italian means "fried mix," and in Venice, the things you mix are small fish and seafood. Kind of like French fries, if they were Italian and came from the sea. I also liked the *Cicchetti,* because depending on where you ordered it, you could end up having all kinds of different things. There was usually a selection of sandwiches, plus *polpette,* which are fried balls of meat, tuna, cheese, or potatoes. All you had to do was remember that one word, *cicchetti,* for a plethora of different snack treats. You could even make a game out of it. *Guess what's in the cicchetti today!*

I know that Tiramisù is the most famous Italian dessert, but my favorite one is gelato. Now, I know most Americans think that "gelato" is just Italian for ice cream, but believe me my friend, that is not true. Gelato is an entirely different experience.

Gelato is creamier, silkier, and smoother than ice cream. Its flavor is definitely more intense. And it's usually served just a few degrees warmer than ice cream, which makes it melt faster and more deliciously in your mouth.

So what makes gelato so much better?

Technically, it has to do with the proportion of milk to cream in the recipe, but that can't be the whole reason. Maybe it's because it's handmade. Maybe it's because making gelato is considered a highly-skilled craft. Some people say that in Venice, gelato is taken as seriously as wine. They make about a million flavors, each with a rich and pure flavor. If you order a mango gelato, you can feel the cool, soft mango melting into your mouth, bringing a euphoria of joy to your taste buds.

We found a gelato shop near the park, so I would get a couple of scoops and devour it while Cowboy sniffed around and did his thing. This meant I ate a whole heck of a lot of gelato. Lemon, pistachio, tiramisù, cinnamon, coconut, and hazelnut—but my favorite was *stracciatella*, which is God's own version of vanilla chocolate chip. Every so often while I was stuffing myself, Cowboy would stop and look up at me, and then I'd give him a little bite. Yes, he licked it off the same spoon I was using. Yes, I know that is gross, but we were on vacation so—no rules. Cowboy likes ice cream, but he is also a gelato fanboy.

Venice would have been more fun with Eva, though. Taking a gondola ride with Cowboy is just not as good as taking one with a beautiful girl on your arm. Holding hands with Eva while walking around this magical city, I could have still had one hand free to hold my gelato. We could have taken a gondola ride to a nice restaurant with outdoor seating, and with her I might have tried one of those seven-course meals that are so customary in Venice. We could have strolled back to our hotel, and enjoyed a nightcap from our balcony. I liked eating gelato with Cowboy, but as cute as he was, his conversation could be lacking.

After Venice, the next stop on our trip was Limone Sul Garda, a town perched on the western shores of Lago de Garda. As we approached it, all I could see were sheer cliffs, rising up from the lake. *Where is this place anyway?* I asked myself. *There's no way they could build anything on those cliffs.* Not to mention, we had to drive through several tunnels just to get there. Before those tunnels were built, the only way to access the town was either by water or over the mountains.

I was beginning to think we'd been lied to, when out of nowhere…Limone Sul Garda appeared. It was built on the only patch of land that wasn't swallowed up by the mountain, its buildings packed closely together in the limited space. Despite this, it still felt open and airy, partly due its large central *piazza*. It had a beach and walking paths all along the water, and most of the restaurants looked out over the lake.

Of course, Cowboy's central concern was locating a suitable place for a pee—and before we could do that, we first had to park the car. *Easier said than done.* As soon as we entered the town, the modern road we'd been travelling on turned into a network of medieval alleyways. *No problem,* I thought to myself. *I've been on worse roads.*

I spoke too soon.

Next thing I knew, the road ended because the center of town was blocked off for pedestrians. I had to turn around and park in a garage way on the edge of town, miles away from our hotel. At that point, Cowboy had been holding his pee in for hours, and I could tell he was getting desperate. He started to lift his leg up on the pillar in the garage. "NO, Cowboy!" I scolded him. "We gotta find some grass!"

The problem was, there *was* no grass. This gorgeous lake town was even worse than Venice. We patrolled the village at top speed, hurrying past the ancient medieval buildings and the famous frescoes. We ignored all the lake views. I couldn't care less about the hotel. I just wanted to find Cowboy a place to pee.

Finally, we spotted it: just fifty feet away was a tall metal light post, and it was surrounded by...*a circle of grass.* Cowboy sprinted to his destination.

Just as he was lifting his leg, a policeman started yelling at us. *"Vietati cani sull'erba!"* he hollered, hurrying over with an angry look on his face. *"Vietato!"*

I held up both hands in surrender. "He just needs a place to pee really fast!"

But the cop crossed his hands in front of his chest. *"VIETATO."*

Cowboy was looking up at me, practically vibrating with his urgent need to pee. "If he poops I'll clean it up, I promise!" I wheedled.

But the cop was having none of it. "NO!"

"Okay," I conceded. "Sorry." I pulled Cowboy away from the light post and headed straight back to the parking garage. As soon as we were out of sight of the police officer, I took Cowboy over to a pillar and told him to pee. I think he must have emptied a gallon on that poor old pillar, and the look of relief on his face was heartbreaking.

That night for dinner, I found a restaurant on the lake with an outdoor patio. We ordered the meat sampler for two, and I split it with Cowboy. Both ours eyes became wide as saucers when we saw the waiter bring it out. Cowboy's butt started wiggling and I'm fairly sure my tongue was hanging out. It had pork chops, lamb chops, steak, chicken sausage, salami, prosciutto, and pepperoni. I think it even had some wild boar on it.

We were a long way from canned Raviolos.

I split that platter fifty-fifty with Cowboy. I would take a bite, then cut him a piece and give it to him. It takes longer to eat that way, but we weren't in a hurry. Several people looked at us like we were crazy, but I didn't care. After dinner, we walked around for a bit and then found a gelato shop on the beach where we shared a scoop of coconut and a scoop of cinnamon.

The last part of the tour of Lago de Garda was not actually on Garda but above it, in a town called Ledro. We drove to the north side of the lake, where the road wound up for miles, climbing and climbing past multiple switchbacks. We ended at a smaller lake at the very top of the mountain, and from there we could admire Lago de Garda, spread out below.

Ledro was magnificent, and this time even Cowboy agreed. Because after all those ancient cities with all those stone paths, after all those cobblestone streets and concrete *piazzas*, after all those angry policemen who wouldn't let Cowboy pee when he needed to go...we finally found it.

Ledro, it turned out, was pee-vana. The palatial gardens of potty. The tranquility of tinkle. The wonderful world of wiz. This town was one giant doggy pee-pee place. We could step outside our hotel and immediately find a dog-friendly patch of grass.

And as to the hikes, there was nothing but nature. This place was so dog friendly that it even received the 2011 recognition of Common Animal Friendly award from the International Tourism exchange in Milan.

So I guess you could say that between Cowboy and me, our reviews of Italy were mixed. I was a big fan of the colorful architecture, the delicious dinners, and the glorious gelatos. But as for Cowboy? He was just thrilled to find a great place to wiz.

GOAT DOG

There is a legend that sprang up from the depths of Les Salles-sur-Verdon, the deepest canyon in France. Some say this canyon is so deep, it nearly touches Hell.

The people whisper that once, a man who was digging for gold went too deep, accidentally opening a fissure that allowed the Goat Dog to escape.

But I saw it myself.

When the great pit opened, demons poured out from within, threatening to inflict suffering and death upon the world. That was when an angel came down from the heavens to drive those demons back. He fought them all, casting them back to their accursed home.

After ridding the world of demons, the angel sealed up the fissure to make sure no more could escape. But before returning to heaven, he looked back. He could not believe how majestic the canyon was, both beautiful and treacherous. So beguiled was he by its beauty that he wished to remain and explore its mysteries. To do so, he donned a disguise. The angel chose a form that was part dog, to let those who saw him know that he was both loving and fierce; and part goat, to enable him to climb the canyon's treacherous walls.

At this time, Goat Dog turned to me. "Wilt thou join me to explore the canyon?" he inquired.

Naturally, I could not refuse a request from an angel. And so I uttered, "Sure, my name's Randy. What should I call you?"

And the Goat Dog spoke, "Cowboy."

Next thing I knew, Cowboy and I were standing at a place called Chalet de la Maline, which was the starting point of this really deep canyon in France. He asked if I'd heard of it before, and I was a little surprised. I thought since he was an angel he'd know everything.

"It's the Sentier Martel hiking trail," I told him. "Dummy."

So off we went, me and an angel named Cowboy. Before long, the path got a little tricky. "You sure you can hack this, Cowboy?" I asked him. "You're looking a little trembly there from that fight with all them demons. I sure would hate it if you slipped and fell." Plus, I imagine God would be pretty upset with me if I let one of his angels die after he just saved humanity from demons and hellfire. I asked if it would be okay to put a harness on him, and the angel Cowboy complied.

But Cowboy surprised the heck out of me. Even though he was weak from fighting a legion of demons, Cowboy did great. That Goat Dog was climbing over obstacles, scrambling past rockslides, and trotting up and down stairs. Nothing could stop him.

The trail was only about ten miles long, but it had so many ups and downs that I felt like I was on a yo-yo. We passed through caves, along the edges of cliffs, and we even stopped to swim in the water at the bottom of the canyon. Cowboy was treading water with me one minute, and the next thing I knew he was perched on the top of a large boulder. "How'd you do that, Cowboy?" I asked.

And Cowboy replied, "I am Goat Dog."

By the time we finished our hike at Point Sublime, people were whispering about the Goat Dog they had glimpsed on the trail. No two of them told the same story. Some said he came from the pits of Hell; others were certain he'd fought an army of demons led by Lucifer himself. Everyone did agree on this: Goat Dog could climb any peak.

And that is how the legend of Goat Dog was born.

Over the next few weeks, there were other sightings of Goat Dog, but I knew they couldn't be true. Because that night the Goat Dog had dinner with me, and the next day we hauled ass back to Switzerland.

007

Oh my God, every road I take is blocked off. The GPS says turn right, but that's a joke because it's closed. What the hell is going on? The hotel's gotta be around here somewhere, but I can't get to it. What the heck's the point of a GPS if all the roads are shut down? WHAT IS GOING ON HERE? Is it a terrorist attack? Why is everything so crowded? Oh God, I'm never gonna make it to the hotel. Poor Cowboy can feel the stress, and now he's starting to whimper. This fool GPS is useless and now I'm just wandering aimlessly around in my car. I've been in this city for just over an hour now, and I'm totally, helplessly lost.

This is crazy. I should have known it was a bad idea to come here. First off, finding a room was just about impossible. Everything was booked for some reason. The only option was a pricey room at the Fairmont, and I decided to take it because this could be my only chance to visit Monaco and Monte Carlo.

More road blocks are sealing off the road to my hotel. Some guy in a uniform is telling me I have to take my bags and *walk* the rest of the way. He says he'll park my car outside of town. *Sure buddy, that's a good one. What kind of a scam is he trying to pull?*

But then other people start giving up their cars, so I figure, *what the heck.* I repack all my essentials into one suitcase, toss the guy my keys, grab Cowboy, and start walking.

Eventually, once I get into the swing of things, I start paying attention to the signs. I was so stressed out trying to get here that I hadn't noticed them before.

FORMULA 1 GRAND PRIX DE MONACO, reads one, and there's a picture of a screaming red race car.

Holy smoke. That's why I couldn't get a room.

I don't need to read French to figure this one out: tomorrow's the opening day of the Monaco Grand Prix.

The roads are shut down because starting in about 16 hours, they'll be part of the most famous racetrack in the world. In fact, the Grand Prix's going to race *right in front of my hotel.*

Wow, this is awesome! I feel like James Bond. Cowboy I spend the evening strolling around to all the famous tourist spots. Cowboy isn't allowed into the Monte Carlo Casino, so I leave him outside and run in real quick to check it out. As far as I can tell, it looks like all the other casinos I've been in. I'm guessing the big difference is the price to play with all those billionaires in the room. Anyway, I'm way underdressed, so I don't mind not playing. The hotel already took most of my money, and I don't need to give the casino the rest of it.

The next morning, I'm yanked awake by powerful engines roaring past the hotel. I hurry to the window, and there they are: dozens of Formula One racecars, tearing around in the streets below.

After taking Cowboy for a walk and enjoying a warm croissant and coffee, I decide to hunt up a better vantage point to check out the races. The hotel has a rooftop pool with all the amenities you'd expect from a fancy hotel in downtown Monte Carlo, so I leave Cowboy in the room and head up to check it out.

When I get there, the pool area's roped off, and there's a grouchy-looking bouncer blocking the entrance. *"Non monsieur,"* he growls, then switches to heavily-accented English. "VIP only on ze terrace."

"Really?" I coax, trying to sound pitiful. "I'm just here for the morning. Do you think I could check it out, just for a few minutes? I promise I won't stay for long."

"Non monsieur," he repeats, unmoved by my sob story. "No one goes in without a pass."

Oh well, it was worth a try. I give him a big Texas smile. "That's okay, I know you're just doing your job. I hope you have a wonderful day!" And with that, I turn to head back down the stairs.

Well, I don't know if this guy is used to difficult people causing a scene, but when I'm polite and friendly with him, he looks shocked. *"Attendez,"* he says, holding up a hand. Then he reaches into his pocket and pulls out...*a VIP rooftop pass.*

"Have a good time," he says, and winks.

Turns out, the rooftop vantage point is even more amazing than I imagined. Here I am, at the top of the Fairmont, in downtown Monte Carlo, VIP pass in hand, watching the Monaco Grand Prix with some of the wealthiest people in Europe. I know these folks have money, because they're wearing jewels to go swim in the pool. I'm a little worried they might drown from the weight of all that gold they've got on. I'm just about blinded by the sparkles.

So I lower my shades, lean against the bar, and marvel at my good luck. *Hot damn. What an amazing bunch of coincidences.*

I feel like ordering a dry martini, shaken not stirred. But I don't drink at all these days, so instead I have a Coke on ice. It's the most glamorous drink I've ever tasted.

FÁE! FÁE!

Years ago when my grandpa died, we found an old letter addressed to his dad from his uncle who lived in Greece. My mother was intrigued. Her grandfather had emigrated from Greece as a young man, and she'd always wanted to search out the Greek side of her family. That letter was our first clue.

Well, I took a copy of the letter and started to dig. It took many hours and hundreds of random emails, but I finally found my mother's cousin Aleka and her husband Apostolis. Not only that, some of their relatives remembered my great-grandpa from when he still lived in Greece!

My mother has been writing them letters ever since.

After my father died, my mom and my Aunt Nanner decided to come back to Switzerland and see me. And of course, this was their big chance: they had to go to Greece and meet the family.

All those stories we hear in the US about Greek hospitality are absolutely true. Just like in the movies, Loula the matriarch kept piling our plates high with moussaka, dolmades, and souvlaki. *"Fáe, fáe!"* she kept urging us, which means "Eat, eat!" And she didn't have to ask us twice. All the food was fresh, homemade, and incredible. We gained so much weight while we were there.

Most of our Greek family didn't speak much English and we didn't speak any Greek, so Apostolis and his sons, Giannis and Nodas, did the translating.

I never felt like a guest with those folks. Despite having never met one another, and even though we were separated by an ocean, we were family. My mother, my aunt and I felt loved and included from the first minute we saw them.

Then, there was the Big Fat Greek Wedding. And I'm not talking about the movie. This was the real deal. Nodas was getting married to Chrysafoulis in the Sanctuary of Agios St. Nikolaos.

"Randy! Come to meet cousin Dimitris."

"Randy! Come to meet little Konstandina and Angeliki."

"Randy! Come to meet uncle Yiorgos and wife Eleni."

Every time I turned around, I was constantly meeting new family members. The ones who couldn't speak English just gave us a hug and a great big smile. The kids tugged on my arm to show me their favorite toys, and the grown-ups were constantly passing plates of *mezze* and urging us to "Fáe! Fáe!"

After the wedding, we drove to a place called Super Kalafatis Beach Restaurant in Galaxidi, where we were greeted by tables piled high with lamb, stuffed grape leaves, spanakopita, dolmades, some kind of bread with multiple dips, and a never-ending supply of drinks. Those Greeks danced all night long, and the food just kept on coming.

By 2:30 a.m. I was exhausted, but the party was just getting started. Finally I couldn't see straight anymore, so I said my excuses and left. I hope I didn't offend anyone, but I just can't party like those Greeks can.

AGGIES

In 1836, Texas defeated Mexico at the Battle of San Jacinto: the final, bloody battle of the Texas Revolution. And on April 21st each year, on the anniversary of the battle, graduates of Texas A&M gather together, wherever they are, to commemorate fellow Aggies who died during the past year.

It's a cool tradition, and it's been happening since 1903. On April 21st, no matter where you are in the world, if there's an A&M Aggie within a hundred miles of you, you're expected to get together, eat a little, sup a little, and live over the days you spent at A&M College of Texas. We call it "Muster."

And in Switzerland, there were some pretty amazing places to muster.

One year, Cowboy and I headed to Zermatt for the ceremony. Zermatt's a picturesque little ski village, nestled in the foothills of the Swiss Alps, and I was excited to see it. The only problem was, we weren't allowed to drive there.

We made it as far as the town of Tasch, where we parked at the train station. So why did we take a train for the last few miles, you may ask, when we had a perfectly functional car? Well, I'll tell you why: you can't drive a car in Zermatt. You can get around on foot, by cable car, and even horse-drawn carriages, but no cars. They work very hard at providing an authentic mountain experience, and I have to say, they do a great job. The place looks like a Christmas postcard. It is located in the upper end of a valley and surrounded by some of the tallest peaks in Switzerland, including Monte Rosa, Dom, Liskamm, Weisshorn, and of course the Matterhorn. Every direction you look, you see mountains. You are in the heart of the Swiss Alps. And with tourism being the main source of income, the entire town is focused on providing an authentic Swiss experience. It was still snowy in April, so they had lots of hot chocolate, hot punch, and Glühwein. And as to Cowboy, he was gratified to discover that they served just about every kind of sausage known to man.

I cannot describe the beauty of our train ride into Zermatt. And that's not because it was so magnificent—I *literally* can't describe it. There was a blizzard that day, and the train was in whiteout conditions. I was actually really glad that I didn't have to drive my car.

Once the train pulled into the station, Cowboy and I got off and started searching for our hotel. Dragging a suitcase with a dog in the snow wasn't fun, but it turned out to be worth it. The hotel wasn't fancy, but that's what made it so wonderful. It was a centuries-old manor house that had been converted into a hotel, and it had probably been owned by the same family for centuries. They made sure everything was perfect, from the knotty pine walls, to the snowy embroidered pillowcases, to the cheerful wood fires in every room.

That night, we met up at the hotel with the other Aggies who were in town for muster. Cowboy and I were the first ones at the meeting place. It was not long before others started joining us. Some of them were recent graduates, and some of them were old like me. The coolest part about muster is that we greeted each other not as strangers, but as old friends who hadn't seen each other in a long time. After everyone had joined and we all said our hellos, a woman named Marianne led us to our restaurant for dinner. And that's where I encountered the glory that is the traditional Swiss Rösti. Something like a bacon-egg-and cheese that is assembled by the angels, the Swiss Rösti goes something like this:

First, there is a layer of golden hash browns pressed together to form a cake. Fried eggs are placed on top of that, so that the golden yolk from the egg spills into the hash browns with every bite. Next there are a couple of pieces of mouthwatering bacon slices, and the whole thing is topped off with a layer of gooey melted cheese, sourced from a farm in a nearby village.

That was one meal I didn't share with Cowboy (except for a small piece of bacon.) I don't think he minded though. He was curled up next to the fire, chewing on a fresh bone I'd bought him earlier, while the feathery snow drifted softly outside. Our group of Aggies talked and reminisced, because in addition to sharing the experience of A&M, we were all Americans who had adventures to share from our time in Switzerland.

After filling up on food and drink, we decided we should walk a little before going to bed. We left the warm fire and headed out into the snow, where the streets were lined with enticing little shops, selling everything from traditional cuckoo clocks to cowbells. With every window we passed, someone had to go inside and check it out. After filling our backpack with souvenirs and chocolate, Cowboy and

I finally decided it was time to go home to bed so that we would be rested in the morning.

The next morning was a clear, brilliant day with the sun shining and birds singing. I was walking along, encouraging Cowboy to pee in the snow. Then I looked up and saw it. Right there, soaring up above me, was the towering peak of the Matterhorn.

It was so cool.

I mean this was THE Matterhorn. The same thing you see on the cover of Toblerone chocolate. It's one of the deadliest peaks in Europe, and has claimed the lives of over 500 alpinists. When you mention Switzerland, this is one of the top things that people think about, and there I was at its base, looking right up at it, staring at the sun glistening off its snowy peak.

Later, I told my new friends about it, and Marianne burst out laughing. "This is nothing, Randy," she assured me. "Wait 'till you get to the top of the Gornergrat and we go out on the observation deck! From there you can look straight across at the Matterhorn!"

I figured Marianne had some pretty high standards for scenery, but I didn't argue. Then we boarded the train for the Gornergrat summit. And that's when the views started getting incredible. I kept snapping pictures, and Marianne kept laughing. "Don't waste your time!" she teased me. "These trash mountains are nothing compared to what's coming up!"

Eventually, we got to the last stop. Marianne led me behind the observation deck and over to a slippery trail. I followed her up a steep path, clutching the guard rails, but Cowboy raced ahead without a problem. He yanked on his leash, eager to take in all the new smells.

Finally we arrived at the summit. And though it pains me to say it, Marianne was right. From that vantage point, we had a panoramic view of more than *twenty* thirteen-thousand-foot peaks, including Dufourspitze, Liskamm, and the Weisshorn And right in between them, its craggy peak splitting the heavens, soared the Matterhorn.

Finally, Marianne pulled out her camera. I just stood there and gaped. The view was indescribable. And that was where we honored our fallen friends from Texas A&M, the Aggies we lost, in the year 2014.

THE DAY COWBOY GOT OLD

We were in a little town called Étretat, up in the northwest of France. Étretat is famous for these sculptural rock formations along the coast, where the Atlantic waves have carved and shaped the cliffs over millions of years. We'd planned a 12-mile hike along the coast to a lighthouse.

Cowboy and I had never turned back from a hike because we were tired. Sometimes if it was unsafe, or if I tried to walk off a cliff, we might head home early—but never just because we were tired. But that day, as the hike wore on, I noticed Cowboy was getting slower. I wanted so badly to make it to the lighthouse, so I kept pushing my buddy. But at one point, he just lay down and refused to go any further.

At that point, I knew our long hikes were done. Cowboy was getting old.

I let him rest. I stood over him, blocking the sun while he had some water. We turned around and headed home, taking it slow and giving him lots of breaks.

After that day on the Normandy coast, we still had plenty of amazing hikes, but they were shorter. We stopped doing 12-mile hikes, but we did eight-mile hikes for a while. Then we dropped down to six, then four, then two. Eventually we stopped hiking together, and I just took my buddy on short walks. I always made sure our excursions weren't too hard. And when it was time to turn back, we did.

BIRTHDAY

September 6th was always a special day for me and Cowboy. It happened to be both our birthdays, and it was also the anniversary of the day I adopted him.

We didn't just do one party—we celebrated all week. In Switzerland, Cowboy and I had a little tradition where we would head to a lake near a town called Titisee, out in the middle of the Black Forest. There was a hotel where we liked to stay, perched right on the lake, with a huge breakfast buffet that included real, crispy, American-style bacon. Cowboy always had an extra helping of bacon.

Then we'd head up into the mountains and hike for the day, eating our lunch by a pond we'd discovered together. The pond was surrounded by trees and colorful flowers, making the reflections in the water look like a Monet painting. A few fallen logs stretched out into the pond, and we sometimes climbed out onto them, balancing on their precarious limbs. A small stream fed into the pond, creating a little beach in the clearing. I laid out part of a yoga mat that I had rolled up in my backpack, and Cowboy and I settled in right next to the water. That way, when he felt hot or was thirsty, he could just go for a swim. That was our special birthday place, and when we left we were always smiling and at peace.

2017 was a special year. Cowboy was turning 91 and we'd been buddies for 12 years. But I wasn't sure we could go to our special mountain pond anymore. Cowboy had hip issues by then, and he just couldn't hike like he used to. He still loved going for walks, but it couldn't be for long, and no climbing mountains. That pretty much ruled out Titisee.

But that year, I also had Eva by my side, and she was full of ideas. While I was still trying to figure out how to make Titisee fun for Cowboy, she took a different approach and started looking for different options. Eventually, she found a little country chalet in France with a nice big fenced-in backyard. It was hard to break our tradition, but that chalet turned out to be perfect.

Every day of that trip, we got up in the morning and took Cowboy for a walk. When he got tired, we went back to the chalet for a rest. I gave him a nice big treat that would take a few hours to eat, and a couple of bowls of water. Then Eva and I would go off on a bigger hike while Cowboy relaxed in the sun. Each night, we sat outside with him and barbecued steaks and sausages on the grill. After that, I built a big fire and we sat out there for hours, chatting and rubbing Cowboy's belly.

It was hard for me to go hiking without Cowboy, even though I knew it was too painful for him by then. We'd been in Europe seven years, and we'd never been separated before. I still feel guilty about it. I hope when I get to heaven, he tells me that what we did was best and he was happy.

On September 6th, Cowboy got his own personal birthday steak. Eva and I also gave him a ton of presents, including a squeaky toy in the shape of a pizza, and a huge bone from the local French butcher. Cowboy was a spoiled dog, and I loved making him happy.

LAST HIKE

I'm at work when Eva calls me. "Randy? I think something's wrong with Cowboy. Can you come home? Just to be safe."

When I get there, Cowboy's lethargic but he doesn't seem too sick. He doesn't want to go for a walk, but he lies down next to me and keeps me company as I start my laptop to continue working from home. Eva goes out to her job, and everything seems all right.

But then, during a meeting, Cowboy starts shaking and panting. "I gotta go, guys," I tell my colleagues. "Right now."

I lie down next to Cowboy and pet him. "It's okay, Buddy," I tell him, though I'm not at all sure that's true. "You're gonna be A-okay."

When Eva gets home, she sits down next to us and Cowboy lays his head in her lap. It's already late, but we decide to call the vet. He comes over and gives Cowboy a shot to calm him down and take away the pain. "You should consider," he tells us gently, "that it is time now. I can help him go without pain." Then he packs up and tells us we can call him as late as we want, if we decide to do it.

What a difficult decision. I don't want Cowboy to suffer, but I don't want to kill him either. In my heart, I know it is time. He's reached the point where he hurts all the time, and he can't do the things he loves most.

I'd always imagined this moment would be different. I thought I would have more time. I thought I could have one last steak with him. If I had to say goodbye, I thought we could do it in the park on the grass, not on our kitchen floor. But it was time now.

I held my buddy close, and Eva called the vet.

* * *

Afterwards, when it was all over and Cowboy had been cremated, we had to decide what to do with his ashes. Cowboy is both Texan and Swiss, so I wanted to make sure that some of his remains stayed in Switzerland and some went back home with me to Texas.

I wanted to give Cowboy a little ceremony, something to reflect all the adventures and fun we had together. And I knew where we had to do it: our special mountain pond, deep in the Black Forest, near the town of Titisee. The place where we always had our special birthday lunch, before Cowboy's hips got too painful to hike.

Yep, that was where a part of him needed to be.

* * *

Eva and I got to Titisee on a Friday evening, and spent some time walking around town. It felt strange not having Cowboy with me. I didn't need to find any grass for him to pee on. I could go into shops without finding a nice shady place for him to wait.

But it was so empty.

I was so glad Eva was there with me. I didn't have Cowboy's leash to hold, but I had Eva's hand. I didn't have Cowboy by my side, but I did have Eva. I don't think I would have made it without her.

Eva started up a funny little habit, right after Cowboy died. All of a sudden, she developed a tremendous craving for ice cream and she needed me to walk her to a handmade gelato place for a scoop. She didn't want to drive, and she didn't want the store-bought stuff; we always had to walk to someplace special. Of course, she wasn't doing it for the ice cream. She did it to keep my mind off Cowboy.

Saturday morning after breakfast, Eva and I set out on our hike. Cowboy was still with us, but this time he was in a box in my backpack. After a few hours, we approached the little pond that was so special to Cowboy and me. It appeared out of nowhere. One minute we were surrounded by trees, then all of a sudden they opened up and before us was this beautiful body of water, glimmering in the sun. All sorts of birds gathered that day singing to us, finches, sparrows, and pipits, creating a symphony music, welcoming us to our special spot. It was peaceful, just as I'd remembered.

My stomach tightened. I was hurting so bad, but I knew this was a special place for my buddy, and I was a glad I could leave a little bit of him there.

As I looked out over the pond, I thought to myself, *This is it. This is our last hike together. Once I bury his ashes I will never again have my buddy with me when I go out hiking, or do anything else. This our last hike.*

I started crying. It was hard, but I knew he would be happy here.

I looked around and found the perfect spot, a tree that grew out over the water. I dug a hole and placed his ashes inside. Eva and I lit a candle, and we said a few words of farewell. Eva then held me and we sat there in silence. The only sound was the water, rippling against the shore.

When I was ready, we got up to leave. I looked at the place where we buried his ashes. "Goodbye, Buddy," I told him. "I'll miss you, and I'm so sorry this is our last hike."

As I turned to leave, the wind picked up. It whispered through the trees, swept out over the water, and as it blew against my face I heard a voice inside my head say, "Randy, I will always be with you in your heart. As long as I am there we will always be together, so it's not our last hike, just the last one in different bodies."

Never underestimate the love of a dog.

THUMP

After Cowboy died, Eva convinced me to take her on a two-week motorcycle tour of the mountain passes of Switzerland and Italy. That's something I would never have done while Cowboy was alive. He liked his throne seat in the front of my car, and there wasn't anywhere for him to ride on a bike.

I don't have a big touring bike, but it's big enough: a Harley Davidson Sportster 1200c. It's probably better suited for in-town trips and weekend excursions, but that bike got us everywhere we wanted to go.

The first challenge was packing. If I thought packing a backpack for one man and a dog was complicated, that was nothing compared to two grown adults on a motorcycle. The night before we were supposed to leave, Eva and I stayed up late, trying to decide what we absolutely had to take with us. Saturday morning, I got up early and had a heck of a time getting everything secured on my bike. I have never had my motorcycle loaded that heavy before.

When I was satisfied that everything was secure, we finally got on the bike and left. We almost fell over pulling out of the driveway. Not only was I not used to having a passenger, but it also had a completely different feel with all that heavy luggage on board. To make matters worse, Eva had a migraine and she'd taken a pill that made her sleepy.

That wasn't really a problem, until we were going 75 miles an hour and I felt Eva sliding off the motorcycle. I kept one hand on the handlebar and reached back to grab her with the other hand to keep her from falling off. We must have looked crazy to the cars around us. *Who's the nutjob on a motorcycle driving with one hand and holding his passed-out passenger with the other?*

I pulled over as fast as I could to wake her up. "Eva!" I shook her. "EVA! Are you okay?!"

"What?" she asked woozily. "I'm fine. Why did we stop?"

"Um, because you almost slid off the bike just now. Are you okay to ride? You're not gonna fall asleep again, are you?"

Eva shook her head. "No, of course not. I'm fine!"

Spoiler alert: she was not fine.

We took off again, and we'd been driving for about twenty minutes, when all of a sudden: THUMP! Something hit the back of my helmet.

It was Eva's helmet. She'd fallen asleep again and slumped forward, hitting her helmet into mine. I reached back and grabbed her as she started to fall to the side.

Once again, I pulled over. I started hunting through my saddlebag.

"What are you doing?" Eva wanted to know. "I just packed those."

"I'm looking for rope," I told her, truthfully. "I figure maybe if I tie you on this time, you won't slip off and die the next time you fall asleep."

"*Rope?*" Eva repeated. "You are not going to tie me with rope. I don't even feel tired anymore. See?" She opened her eyes wide and smiled. "I am fine."

Well, I couldn't tie her up if she wouldn't let me, so I bought her an energy drink and made her drink it. Eventually we managed to get to Geneva where we stopped for the night without any major problems, but she was worn out and hurting badly. Can you imagine riding on the back of a motorcycle with a migraine? That must have been horrible.

If we thought Saturday was scary, it was nothing compared to Tuesday. We had two mountain passes to get through that day, the Albula pass and Splügen Pass. That morning, we woke up to the sound of rain: never a good sign when you're on a motorcycle.

At first, it didn't seem too bad. The rain was annoying, but it wasn't dangerous for driving. Then we started to head up into the mountains. The higher we got, the colder it was and the less visibility we had. After awhile, we were both freezing and miserable.

Then we got into the clouds, and the visibility went down to almost zero. By the time we started going over the pass, I was watching the lines on the road next to my feet to guide my way. There was a wall on one side of us and a sheer drop-off on the other. Not to mention, this was a Swiss pass, and hairpin turns came out of nowhere. It would have been a tough day in sunny conditions. I was nervous, but Eva must have been terrified. She was squeezing me so tight, I had a hard time breathing.

Finally, we made it to the other side of the pass and I looked for a place to pull over and catch our breath. Eva took off her helmet, and that's when I saw that she was crying.

"How did you do it?" she asked between sobs. "I thought we were definitely going to die!"

"Oh my love," I told her, grabbing her in a big hug. "I know it was hard, but I was being safe."

"But *how could you see?!*"

I told her how I followed the lines on the road.

"But I couldn't even see *you*, how did you see the lines?!"

It took me a minute, but eventually I realized what had happened. Eva rode the entire trip with her visor all the way closed. Of course it fogged up and she couldn't see a damn thing. She'd assumed that I'd been as blind as she was.

"No my love," I told her. "I lifted my visor up. It was cold and wet, but at least I could see. I *promise* I could see!"

That story makes me laugh now, but can you imagine riding on the back of a motorcycle going over a dangerous mountain pass, thinking the driver had no visibility? What kind of faith did she have in me that she didn't jump off the bike, yelling, "OH HELL NO!"

Luckily the rain let up soon after and the sun came out. The rest of the day turned into a great day for riding. After the Splügen pass we crossed into Italy, where we stayed the night at Lake Como. We walked around the lake, we both ate gelato, and nobody fell off a mountain.

A LETTER FROM LUNA

Buna ziua everyone!

I hope you are doing well. My name is Luna and I would like to tell you what happened to me this year.

I was at home in my cage in Romania hiding from the other bad dogs when someone dragged me into a scary van. There were other dogs there, and all the dogs were in tiny cages, howling and crying. We had no idea what was happening! Sometimes we would stop, and a man would grab one of us and drag them away. Each time the van stopped, we hid at the back of our cages, hoping the man wouldn't choose us.

We drove for many days, and finally, it was my turn. The man seized me and dragged me out. Then he forced me into a double harness. A collar around my neck and a harness around my waist and shoulders. It was terrible. A prison!

Then I was outside and there were more people, a man and a woman. I knew this was my chance to get away. I snapped at the new man and he stepped back. Then I pulled and wiggled with all my might. I got the collar around my neck off! Ha ha, only one more to go. This one should be easy, and then I can escape.

I nearly freed myself, but nu. This new man was trickier than he looked, a real diavol! I saw the woman who was with him was almost in tears, and I took heart. Maybe I will get away yet!

I pulled the new man into a big mud puddle, thinking surely that would cause him to lose concentration. He reached for me, and I bit him! What, is he nebun?! He just let me bite him. Oh, that tricky man. While biting him, he was able to grab me.

Then I became desperate. I was fighting so hard to escape that I started to do pooping everywhere. Ha! Pooping! Now there's no way this man will catch me, because I know that people are disgusted by dogs pooping. He will have to jump into this mud puddle full of poop and wrestle me to the ground. I am sure to get away.

But this tricky man surprised me. He looked at the poop, he looked at me, he looked at the poop again, he looked back at the woman—and then he jumped into the poop! This man, he is crazy, a real nebun!

We fought. I snapped at him, but he kept coming. We rolled around in the poop for what seemed like forever, but then he had me. That was when the woman rushed over and put the collar back on me. The new man held me to his body and put me into his car.

I was so scared. I could not stop shaking.

The woman was nice. She sat with me and tried to comfort me. She offered me food, but I was too scared to eat. During the ride in the car I learned that the woman was called Eva and the man was called Randy. They kept talking about taking me to my new home. I hoped it did not have bad dogs in it, like the place where I lived before.

Randy and Eva took me into their home, a place that they called "apartment." They wanted me to look around, but I found a corner in the back to hide. This is where I stayed for several days! I did not trust these tricky people.

But Randy and Eva did not get mad. They just kept petting me. They brought food and water, and they talked in soft voices.

That was many weeks ago. Now I call these people Mommy and Dad. I am fericit, happy like a little puppy!

Because of them, I know what it is like to be loved.

Cu drag,
Luna

BABY GIRL

Well, you heard it from her first. In December 2019, Eva and I adopted a four-legged baby girl from Romania.

Originally, it was all Eva's idea. She wanted to get another dog after we lost Cowboy. Enough time had passed, and I felt like I could start accepting the idea of a new dog. I knew Cowboy would want us to keep giving a loving home to other animals. So Eva hit the internet, searching for a rescue dog to adopt.

One day, Eva was on her laptop when she called me over to check out a video. The film quality was grainy and terrible, and it mostly showed a funny-looking dog running away from all the aggressive dogs in her shelter. But this one was different. The other dogs were all very social, wagging their tails, shoving to the front to be seen, and excited to meet new people. Not Luna. She was hunched over in fear, tail between her legs, head down. She was frightened of everyone, always running back to the shelter of the dog house. But Eva didn't care about all that. She was reading the profile, where it said that Luna had been living in the streets, and she'd been in the shelter for five years.

"This is the one," she insisted. "If we do not rescue her, no one else will. She is too ugly. She will live the rest of her life in that shelter, being lonely and afraid. We need to get her and show her love, give her a home and a family."

When we first brought Luna home, she was so full of fear. Her little snout was covered with scars from the dogs in the shelter who'd attacked her, and it was almost impossible to take her for a walk. She was scared of all people, especially men. It was obvious that she had been horribly abused. It took time and a lot of work from Eva, but now Luna is a loving little funball who keeps us laughing every day.

With her first tail wag, Luna started to heal. At first it wasn't much to look at, just a little flicker out at the tip. Then it grew. The flickers got longer and used more and more of her tail. After a while, she'd wag her tail all the time. Eventually, she started wagging her tail so hard that her butt would wag! The first time she flicked the tip of her tail, she melted our hearts. Luna still has some anxiety issues, but Eva does a great job working with her and she gets more confident every day.

Eva says that I'm the only man Luna trusts. Now our baby girl greets me excitedly when I come home from work at the end of the day. I am blessed because not only does she trust me, she loves me—and the feeling is mutual.

We can't wait to take her to the US. We'll get a house with a big backyard that she can play in, and I'll cook her steaks on the grill. She might have had a difficult life so far, but we're going to do everything possible to make sure the rest of her life is awesome.

That's why I love Eva: she has such an amazing heart. She wanted to save the dog that nobody else would.

MAKING IT OFFICIAL

After seven years in Switzerland, it was time to move back to the US—but I didn't want to leave Eva behind. I did some research on the internet, and it turns out that it's pretty complicated to bring your Hungarian girlfriend home with you.

Your Hungarian *fiancée*, however—that's easier.

The only problem was, I didn't have a ring. But my mom did. A silver band interlaced with turquoise, it was a simple but beautiful ring that had belonged to my grandmother. And by an amazing coincidence, that happens to be Eva's favorite color *and* her favorite stone. I knew she would love it.

The first weekend after Christmas, we drove out with Luna to a forest just outside of Kreuzlingen and went for a hike. Towards the end of the hike, I deviated from the main trail onto a smaller one.

"This is not the trail we take," Eva protested.

Trying to keep a straight face, I bluffed. "I know, I just wanted to try something new."

"But why are we going this way"?

"To let Luna sniff new things," I lied.

By this time, Eva knew me well enough that she could tell I was up to something. She just couldn't figure out what it was.

"But how do you know about this trail?" she poked.

"I just happened to spot it on the map, and wanted to give it a try. Look at Luna, she's loving it!" By this time, I was trying to change the subject. I have a hard time keeping a poker face, and I wanted to surprise her.

Finally we got to the spot I'd planned out in advance. Next to the trail was a little clearing, made just for people to stop and take a break. It had a bench near a stream, where you could sit and listen to the water rushing past. It was just big enough for a picnic...or a proposal.

I pulled Eva off the trail and over to the bench. Then I dropped to one knee and brought out the ring.

Eva did a double-take and stared.

"Eva," I began, trying to keep my voice from shaking. "Will you marry me?"

She didn't say anything, but I'm a patient man. I waited.

Then she still didn't say anything. I started to get nervous. Also, my knee was starting to hurt. *Is she trying to let me down easy? What if she says no?*

"Eva?" I repeated. Now Luna was acting weird. She started pacing back and forth and let out a little whimper. I think she was trying to tell Eva, "Come on Mom, let's make this official and we can be a real family!"

Finally, Eva spoke. "Is this a joke?"

"*No,* it's not a joke! I'm down here on one knee with my grandmother's ring! I'm asking you if you'll marry me!"

And that's when Eva started crying. I stood up. "Eva? Did I say something wrong?"

She just shook her head, and hugged me. We stood there together for a long time, Luna racing around us. Finally, I had to break the silence. "Eva?" She looked at me. "Um. You still haven't answered my question?"

And that's when she smiled. "YES!" she said. "*Of course,* I will marry you!"

I've never been so happy in my life, and I think even Luna understood what was happening, because she jumped up on both of us, her tail wagging her little butt like crazy.

It was finally happening. The three of us were going to be a family.

* * *

Later that day I read a report about a strange glow people witnessed in the forest near Kreuzlingen. Some thought it was a UFO, but I know what it really was. After I put that ring on her finger, Eva was glowing for the rest of the walk back to the car.

But I still tease her about how she didn't answer when I asked her to marry me.

2020

There's a dark cloud forming in the east. I can't see it yet, but it's there, and it's getting bigger, and it's coming our way...

EARLY JANUARY

There's so much work to prepare for my transfer back to the States! But that's all right, we're taking care of it. Our flights are booked, we fly out in March and I start my new job in Tempe, Arizona on April 1st!

The clouds are getting bigger, darker, and closer. We're so busy, we don't even notice them—but we should.

MID-FEBRUARY

We've organized the movers to pack up everything in our apartment and ship it back to the States. They'll be here on March 19, the cleaners will come in on the 21st, and the new tenant moves in on March 27! It isn't easy to coordinate an international move, but we got this. We de-registered from living in Switzerland, and we've sent notices to close our bank accounts, cancel our insurance, cancel the internet and all our utilities.

Things look ready to go! We even put down a down payment on an apartment in Arizona. We're both so excited to be moving!

The storm is here, and it is worse than we could ever imagine.

MARCH 11, 2020

We're all set to go! We brought in some snacks and I'm having my going-away party in just a few days.

Then I hear the news. President Trump has closed the borders from Europe to the US. Only Americans and immediate family members are allowed in.

Fiancées don't count.

Things start to get bad. Eva can't go with me. The office is talking about closing. Some people are already in quarantine.

I can't leave my fiancée behind. What do we do now?

As of April, I will no longer have a Swiss work permit. And my new job is in the US. Do I stay in Switzerland with no job and no house? Or do I abandon my family but keep my new job?

Maybe it won't be that bad. Maybe we'll be separated for just a few weeks. I'll go out to the US first, and Eva and Luna can join me later.

I have a really bad feeling about this.

MARCH 18, 2020

Now it's starting to get scary.

Going to the office is no longer allowed. Everyone has to work from home. Borders across Europe are closing. The grocery store shelves are empty. Our flight to the US is canceled.

Eva's from Hungary. She could be deported from Switzerland at any moment.

We still have to move out of the apartment. I work on the move all day, and at night I scour the internet, trying to figure out how to bring Eva with me to the US. Then I have to start cancelling everything: our car rental, our hotel, the apartment in Arizona that we won't be able to live in.

Only one day until the movers come. We are exhausted and beyond stressed out. The clock is ticking, and we still don't know what to do. The flight options are limited, the routes are terrible, and I can't bring myself to click Purchase. That would kill any chance we have of staying together. I can't put into words this desperate nightmare.

Eva and I discuss our options. Could she fly to Mexico, and then join us in the US when the borders re-open? No, Mexico's borders are closed as well. The entire world is shutting down. Do I keep my new job in the US? But then where will Eva and Luna stay? With all the fear of a global pandemic, there aren't many apartments around to rent.

We're starting to give up hope. But then God sends us an angel.

Andy's a German colleague who keeps a little basement studio rental in the neighborhood for when he comes here on business. He won't be back in town for awhile, so he gives us the keys to his apartment! I hardly even know this guy. He shows us the studio, gives us his keys, and then he leaves to go back to Germany.

We're overwhelmed. We were at such a low point, so close to giving up completely. And then Andy just hands us his keys because he sees two people who are desperate for help.

We're standing in his apartment, alone with our dog, when Eva wraps her arms around me and starts bawling. She tells me she had given up. She didn't believe it would work out. Andy's act of kindness has reinvigorated us.

The basement apartment is tiny. It has very little light. It's one room plus a bathroom. The room has a kitchen section, a small table, and a couch that folds out into a bed.

The table is too small for two laptops and a cup of coffee.

Eva gives her lessons on the table while I work on the couch. If I have a meeting, I take it in the bathroom. But at least we have a place to live.

MARCH 19, 2020

The movers are supposed to come today. We don't know if they'll be able to make it. What will we do if they can't come because of Covid? We have to move out because someone else is moving in. I need to leave for the US in two weeks if I'm going to keep my job.

I look at my watch. The movers were supposed to be here an hour ago. I am getting very nervous.

Bad thoughts keep racing through my mind. What will we do if they can't come? What if they do come and pack us up but then they can't get our stuff to the shipping company in Denmark?

They finally show up, three hours late.

I don't remember what time they finished, but it's dark outside when they finally drive away.

MARCH 20, 2020

Down in the basement, I'm desperately trying to figure out what to do.

As the infection rate and the number of deaths increase, I know in my heart that I can't leave my family. I am panicked. I am running out of ideas. I write and call a US senator trying to get her to find a way to bring Eva over. I write and call the White House.

I contact the US Embassy in Bern. Finally, someone picks up the call.

Unfortunately, there isn't much they can do. They tell me if I can get married, they'll help Eva apply for an emergency visa. But how do we get married?

We're both de-registered from Switzerland so we can't get married here. We could get married in Denmark, but the borders are all closed and there's no way to get there. I write and call two state governors, a US district judge, and two US senators.

No one can help.

MARCH 23, 2020

I no longer believe I can bring Eva home with me. I'm devastated. I can't find a reasonable flight so I don't buy a ticket. Maybe nothing looks reasonable because the thought of leaving my family during this crisis is just too much.

Then, another angel appears.

My friend Roland has an idea. Without even telling me, he starts working through SAP headquarters to get special permission for me to continue living and working in Switzerland.

SAP is a massive company, and they're much more persuasive than just one guy acting alone. It feels like a mighty machine had been activated and it's roaring to life, focused on one mission: keeping my family together.

Just the thought of this brings tears to my eyes.

I'm so grateful that SAP cares about people, something you don't see a lot in big companies nowadays.

For the first time in a long time, I have hope.

MARCH 24, 2020

No dice. Our immigration consultants don't think they can reverse my de-registration. Without a work permit, I have to go home.

I'm devastated.

Eva keeps asking what's wrong. She can see it on my face. I can't bring myself to tell her. I am absolutely crushed. It's such a scary time to be separated. I'm terrified of what could happen to Eva when I'm gone. What if she gets sick? Horrible thoughts are flooding my mind.

But SAP isn't finished yet. The machine had been awakened and it's not going to be stopped so easily. Even though I've given up, my friends haven't. Roland, Bernhard, Martin, Dirk, Dagmar, Michal, and all the people in SAP that I don't even know are all pushing and fighting for us.

MARCH 26, 2020

I'm still looking for flights back to the US, and it makes me feel sick. I can't stay here without a work permit. I haven't felt so awful since my dad died.

Then I get an email.

I open it and read the first few lines. "I finally have some good news! My colleagues confirmed they found a way to annul Randy's Swiss work permit de-registration."

SAP has found a way. I try to stand up to show Eva, but I fall to my knees. I'm so overwhelmed with emotion that I can't even stand. Eva rushes to me and asks what's wrong.

I have tears in my eyes and I can barely speak. All I can get out is, "We can stay together, we can stay together."

FOUR-HANDED BELLY RUB

The first of April marked a new chapter in our lives. We knew we could stay together in Switzerland, but that didn't mean life was easy. We were still living out of a suitcase in someone's basement. SAP had declared the offices closed, so I was working from home while Eva continued to teach remotely. It made for long days, the three of us in that dark little flat.

All non-essential stores were forced to close. We could get groceries, but that was it. How are socks and underwear not essential? Maybe if you have a drawer full it's no problem, but I'd only brought a few pairs to save room in my suitcase. We didn't own a bowl and we couldn't go buy one. We needed office supplies, but we couldn't get any.

I don't care what anyone says—socks and underwear are essential.

We did find something that helped us. When one of us got too stressed, we'd shout, "Four-Handed Belly Rub!" Eva and I would then pounce on Luna and give her great big belly rub, all four hands at the same time. It's amazing how much that calmed us all down. Luna's tail would wag, and she'd get all wiggly. The smile on her face would brighten the room for a few minutes. We needed the Four-Handed Belly Rub a lot in those days.

* * *

Then there was the landlord Mateo, who never really liked us. He tolerated us until his nice wife Flurina died, and then he became openly mean to us. I'm not sure what his problem was—maybe it was because we weren't Swiss. When he found out we weren't vacating the flat, he turned into a monster.

One afternoon, Eva and I were working when we heard a knock on the door. It was Mateo. I opened the door with a smile and greeted him, and that's when he started yelling. In his broken English, he demanded that we all had to leave immediately. He ordered us to pack our bags right then and there, in the middle of a global pandemic.

I couldn't believe it. What kind of jerk would do something like this? I told him we couldn't leave, that we didn't have anywhere to go.

He kept right on yelling, in a mixture of German and English. I'm not sure what he said, but at one point Eva started yelling back.

Finally, I convinced him that we would need a few days to find another place. He said that Eva and I could stay a few more days, but Luna had to leave immediately.

"No way," I told him. "We're not kicking our baby girl out into the streets."

So he stormed off, saying we all had to go, or else the dog had to go, or else he was going to call the police.

I called Andy to let him know what was going on, just in case Mateo called him. I didn't want to get Andy in trouble. And somehow, Andy got Mateo to agree to let us stay for awhile.

It's a funny thing about a global pandemic—when the chips are down, people really show their true colors. I find it interesting how some people were so helpful while others were so hurtful. Thankfully, most people helped.

Then there was Luna. I know we said we rescued her, but Eva and I think she was an angel sent by God to help us through those difficult times. She was the one constant that kept us smiling. Taking her out for walks, her wonderful greetings when we came home from shopping, four-handed belly rubs, and all the other little things she did to make us smile.

Luna was our saving grace.

HITCHED

If we were ever going to make it back to the US, we had to get an Emergency Spouse Visa from the Embassy. To do that, we had to get married. To get married, we needed two things. One, an open courthouse that was officiating marriages. And two, we needed all the other government offices to open so we could collect all the documents we needed for the visa.

Only everything was closed.

At the beginning of June, things started rolling again. I was able to schedule an appointment at the Embassy to get a document notarized declaring I was single, which is required under Swiss law. At first, I thought they were joking. What kind of a document proves that you're single? A Declaration of Bachelorhood? But apparently, a lot of countries in Europe use that system, and Eva even had hers already. So with a little Texan know-how, I wrote one myself. Then I took it into the US embassy to get it notarized.

At the embassy, people were grim-faced and serious—at least I *think* they were. It was hard to tell, since they were all wearing masks. A soldier had to verify my passport and my appointment, then I had to empty my pockets and go through a metal detector. Once I was inside, the payment window was sealed and pressurized so that when it opened, a strong wind came rushing out. The official took my money with gloved hands and placed it in a decontamination bin. Then he threw away his gloves in a hazmat container.

The whole interaction was weird, and it made me feel like an infectious biohazard. But eventually, I got my documents, and I was officially single.

Then we were free to plan a wedding date, but nothing was available for weeks. Things just don't move quickly when everything's shut down in a global pandemic. And the wedding was just one step in the process: Eva needed to have an interview with the Embassy, a medical exam by a doctor in Bern, and we still didn't know if she'd get her visa approved.

Did I mention how stressful this was? Every day, we had no idea what would happen to us. Every day, we were fighting to complete all the steps in our quest to move back to the US. Every day, we had no idea what was happening with all our possessions. The shipping company refused to send them until I was physically in the US, so apparently they were being held in a storage facility in Copenhagen. I figured it was entirely possible the company might go out of business from the pandemic and we'd never see any of our stuff again.

Finally, finally, finally, on July 27, Eva and I were allowed to get married.

We didn't have many nice clothes. We had only packed a suitcase each and all the stores were closed because of the pandemic. Eva couldn't even get her hair done. I happened to have packed one blue dress shirt and a pair of khakis, but all I had to wear on my feet were sneakers. Eva had packed a turquoise sun dress and a pair of strappy sandals. It wasn't traditional wedding attire, but it would work. The day of the wedding, I actually braided Eva's hair for her. That was my first time to braiding hair, and I have to admit—it turned out pretty good.

It wasn't exactly the wedding I'd imagined. I always thought my whole extended family would be there, and all my friends from Texas A&M, and we'd have a huge party and reception.

It wasn't like that at all. Only a few of our Swiss friends were allowed to be there, and two of them held up phones to share the ceremony with our families in the US and Hungary. The wedding was done in German, so the officiant would say something and pause for the interpreter to tell me what was said. If I had to respond, I would tell the interpreter who would then tell the officiator.

But even with all that, it was still one of the happiest days of my life. Not only was I marrying the love of my life, but now that we were officially married, it would be much harder for people to break us apart. This really helped ease a lot of stress.

And Eva looked absolutely stunning in that turquoise dress.

.

LAST DAY

It's September 4, the day before we leave. We're ready to go. Our flights are still operating, the hotel is booked, and we're almost packed.

The last thing we need to do is drop Eva off at the doctor's for her immigration physical, and take Luna for one last check at the vet. We're all excited. Even Luna can tell something's going on. She keeps running around in circles, full of nervous energy.

"Tomorrow's gonna be tough," I tell her. "It's going to be a long day of traveling. But after that, everything's going to be great. We're going to get a house with a big backyard that you can run around in. We'll put in a dog door so you can go outside anytime you want. I'm gonna get a big old barbecue so I can grill up some steaks for you whenever we feel like it." I pet her and stroke her until she sighs with contentment. "You're gonna have the happy life you deserve, Luna. I know the first half was tough, but the second half is gonna be awesome."

We all hop in the car and I drop Eva off at the mall next to the doctor's office. Then I drive to the vet. I put Luna in her harness and walk her over to the clinic. When the vet opens the door, I feel the leash go slack, and I look back at my baby girl. She's sitting there on the sidewalk, looking nervous.

And somehow, she's managed to wiggle right out of her harness.

I look at her and say, "No baby girl, please don't." But it's already too late. She takes off running into the street. I sprint after her as fast as I can, waving my arms and trying to signal the cars to stop.

I'm not fast enough. A grey sedan slams right into her, and Lula's little body goes flying. *"Help me!"* I scream, and the vet runs to her side. He picks her up in his arms, blood staining his lab coat, and he brings her inside to his clinic.

I know it's too late. I stand in the street, unable to move. The vet comes out and confirms my worst fear. "I'm so sorry," he tells me. "She is already gone. If there is anything good here, it's that she was hit in the head. She died instantly."

I let out a noise that I don't know how to describe. It's a combination of crying, moaning, and screaming. I have never felt such a tearing, ripping pain in my life. *Our baby girl is dead, the day before we leave.* The doctor takes my arm and leads me inside. I am shaking so badly. The devastation I feel is overwhelming. The doctor gives me some paper towels to wipe the blood and poop off of me. *I was so close to her when it happened. Why couldn't I have been a second faster? Why couldn't I have pulled her to safety?*

I'm supposed to protect her and I failed. I'm supposed to protect Eva and I failed. Oh my God. How am I going to tell Eva her baby girl was killed by a car? I don't know if I can do this. I collapse in the doctor's office. Suddenly, I need to get away. I run outside and stagger aimlessly down an alley. I must sound like I'm dying; people come out of their houses and ask if I'm okay. *I'm not okay; I want to die.* But what can I tell them? "I'm fine," I mumble, and then I start crying again. This terrible keening keeps coming out of my mouth. *How am I going to tell Eva? Please God, please. Make this a dream. Wake me up!*

Luna had such a tough life. She was finally happy. Wagging her little tail, smiling. She was supposed to have at least ten more years of good, happy life. No, it's not fair. God, bring her back to us.

I call my mom, trying to pull together enough strength and composure to be able to tell Eva. *Oh my God, I can't do this. Please Lord, please. Bring her back.* My mom has never heard me this upset before. She tries to comfort me but she mostly listens. I can tell she's fighting to keep from bursting into tears. She wants to be there for me, and it's killing her that she can't.

It's different from when Cowboy died. He had a good life and it was time for him to go. Luna had suffered for most of her days, and we were supposed to give her a happy life. *I failed her. This just can't be happening. Please God, I will do anything. Make this a dream. Wake me up. Please God. Our poor baby girl.*

The day before we leave. What have I done to make God so angry with me?

I go back to the vet's office to ask if I can bring Eva back to say goodbye. I'm still shaking. They tell me they will keep her for us, but that I should not drive in my condition. They're probably right, but I have to go tell Eva. This will probably be the most difficult thing I will ever have to do. Nothing could have prepared me for it. I go to my car and drive to the doctor's office. Tears are streaming down my face, and it's hard to see the road.

I get to the doctor's and park the car. I'm dying inside. Eva is outside on the sidewalk, waiting for me. I give her a hug and I tell her. She goes into shock. I'm not sure she believes me.

This kind of news is just incomprehensible.

Eva doesn't break down until we get to the vet. Seeing Eva holding her lifeless baby girl while crying is almost too much for me. I want to die.

We make arrangements for the vet to cremate the body and have my friend Roland pick up her remains.

I don't remember the drive home.

When we get home, we're greeted with all the things we'd arranged to bring on the trip for Luna. Treats, toys, and food.

We leave the apartment to return the car, choosing to walk back home. It's so painful. Everything we see has a memory attached.

This is the field where she'd catch her second wind and zoom all over the place.

This is where we'd stop and give her water. It had the best shade after that long stretch in the sun.

Remember how she never wanted to go this way, and I always had to run back and coax her into coming? That one time, I even had to carry her in my arms.

It's all too much to bear. Finishing our packing that day is a colossal chore. All we want to do is sleep and cry, but we can't. We have to catch a flight the next day.

That night in bed, we take turns holding each other and crying. We don't sleep very much at all.

ANGEL

The next day was a fog. Eva and I were like zombies, just going through the motions. Trying to answer questions at all the different airport security checkpoints felt like having our teeth pulled. At check-in, I had to tell the flight attendant that we no longer needed to purchase a ticket for our dog, and I broke down all over again.

He must not have updated the records, because after we boarded, another flight attendant came up to tell us that Luna hadn't been loaded yet. It was like some kind of sick practical joke. Once more I had to explain that Luna had been hit by a car and she was no longer coming with us.

We must have looked horrible, huddled together and crying. They brought us a box of Swiss chocolates and offered us champagne. We accepted the chocolates but I didn't want the champagne. If I started drinking, I was afraid I wouldn't stop.

All that pain and trouble, trying to keep my family together, and to get us all safely to the US. All our dreams were almost achieved. Only one day away, and then BOOM. Something died in me that day. It was all just too much.

God, please let her be in heaven with you. Please let her be happy. Please let her feel no pain, ever again.

Sometimes I'm so angry at God. *How could he do this? Why didn't He protect our little girl?* Other times, I'm so grateful for God. *What if He knew that by preventing her from getting to the US, He was protecting her from something even worse?* And at least she didn't suffer. I still miss Luna so much, but I would rather live with this pain for the rest of my life than have her suffer for even a day.

Eva and I had said all along that Luna was an angel sent to help us through this difficult time. Maybe now that we were finally leaving, God needed her back. I don't know.

What I do know is this: if she was an angel, and she did know it was her time to leave us, she played one last joke on me. The first day we met she got poop on me, and the last time I saw her she got poop on me.

I pray so much that was Luna's little joke, and one day in heaven we'll laugh about it together.

EPILOGUE: THE BEGINNING

We arrived in Tempe with nothing, not ready to start our new life. We were two zombies, going through the motions but not really there.

At first, everything was hard. Trying to make major decisions like buying a house and a car while in a deep depression was overwhelming. We put in an offer on a house that we didn't even want. Thankfully, the inspections showed enough issues that we were able to cancel the contract.

But then, we found the home that was right for us. Eva wanted this house the moment we walked in the back door and saw a bunch of dogs running around and playing in the giant backyard. It's a bit older, and it will require some maintenance, but none of that matters. It's built on a cul-de-sac, right on the edge of a walking trail—so we can take our dogs for a walk without getting near any busy streets. The house also has enough space for two offices, so while Eva and I are both working from home, I won't need to take meetings in the bathroom.

The day after our offer on the house was accepted, we adopted a new rescue dog named Alma.

The first time she saw Eva, Alma sat down in her lap, and claimed Eva as her new mommy. I knew then that we would end up adopting her. Our hearts were so empty, and we needed to do something to fill them or we knew we weren't going to make it.

At first, Alma was afraid of everything, especially me. She hid in a corner the first few days, and she didn't eat much. The first night we took her outside for a walk, she tried to get out of her harness and run away. I jumped on top of her and screamed at Eva to grab her. I've never had a panic attack before, but I think that's what happened to me that night. Eva ended up having to hold Alma's leash for several weeks. I stayed behind them, watching Alma the whole time, just waiting to grab her if she tried to run.

Four months after we arrived back in the States, we received our container full of possessions. We were so excited to get our stuff. The night before the container arrived, I could barely sleep. Alma was wondering what was going on, and what we were both so excited about. When the movers started unloading our furniture, I was like a little kid at Christmas. *Look, it's our bed! Oh my gosh, we got our bed! Put it back in the master bedroom. Oh my gosh, is that our kitchen table? How awesome! That goes here. Plates and silverware and kitchen utensils, oh my! My desk and chair, woo hoo! I can now work comfortably from home and have space for BOTH my laptop and a coffee mug! Clothes, we have clothes! No more laundry every couple of days. Hot diggity damn!*

By that point, we'd lived with so little for so long, getting our stuff was like winning the lottery.

Eventually, we got to the boxes of souvenirs and mementos from Switzerland. Opening those was bittersweet. When we got to the box of stuff we had packed for Luna,

Eva and I both lost it. We unpacked all the practical items right away, but the boxes of souvenirs took us months to work through.

In January, we adopted another rescue dog named Cass.

Cass is a snuggler. He a 50-pound dog who will try to climb into your lap any chance he gets. He has given me a bloody nose and broken glasses with his bountiful, unrestrained face licking. We call Cass our little monster, but we love him. He is energetic, full of life, totally destructive and incredibly sweet.

Both Cass and Alma were rescues from Mexico, and it's obvious that Alma had to fight to survive down there. Even though Cass is younger, stronger, and a whole heck of a lot bigger, Alma can take him down in a blink of the eye. She is amazing to watch. She's got some finely-tuned dog ninja moves. Cass might be the big guy, but Alma's the one I would want next to me in a fight—although mainly I want to make sure she never gets into a fight in the first place.

Despite our two new dogs, Eva still needed to do more to heal from Luna's death, so she decided to spend a month in Mexico working at a dog rescue shelter called Foundation DAR (Defenders of Animals at Risk.) When she came home, she didn't bring me a t-shirt. Instead, she had our third dog—Coconut. That poor guy had it rough. At just a few weeks old, he'd been found next to his dead mother on the street. When Eva met him, he was small, undernourished, and afraid. Upon his arrival in the US, he got so sick we had to take him to the emergency hospital for several days. We weren't sure he was going to make it.

Thankfully, Coconut recovered. He gained 25 pounds and spends his time bounding around our big back yard with his brother and sister. He's also a fan of digging into a nice fat steak when we barbecue.

As with all shelters, the Foundation DAR that Eva worked at is always in need of money to do their work, and of course Eva decided to do something about it. Like I said, she doesn't just feel bad about a problem, she takes action. Eva and I have created a not-for-profit company to raise money for Foundation DAR. We call it DAR Foundation (rescue) and you can follow our efforts here: https://darfoundationrescue.org/

I'm sorry I never got to barbecue for Luna, but I think she'd be happy to see all the steaks our new rescues are eating. The first time I fired up the grill, the dogs weren't sure and stayed way back. After I put the meat on and they could smell it cooking, they ventured a little closer. When we gave them a piece of steak to try, all three were timid about taking it. I guess they thought it was too good to be true, maybe a trap. They sniffed it, they licked it, then finally... they tasted it. After trying the first bite, their hesitation was GONE. Soon they were running in circles, so excited they had a hard time sitting down long enough to eat.

Now every time I fire up the grill, I have three dogs watching me, tongues hanging out of their mouth, tails and butts wagging, and a puddle of drool at their feet. And sometimes, out of the corner of my eye, I swear I can see Cowboy and Luna standing behind them, smiling.

ACKNOWLEDGMENTS

Where do I start? So many wonderful people helped me create this book. There's just no way to list them all.

Thank you to my German class and my teacher Uta. My friends at the Fun-in-Konstanz group and the organizers Sean and Christian.

I am thankful for all the wonderful people who were there for us throughout the Covid-19 pandemic. For all my co-workers who fought to keep us together, my landlord Marcel who supported us so much during the move, Andy who just gave us his key to his basement apartment, JJ and all the wonderful people at the Embassy. Without all of them, we would not have made it. A special thank you to Roland for never giving up, for organizing a way for me to stay in Switzerland with my family, and for being a part of our wedding, along with his family.

The adventure in Switzerland would have not been the same without having my TGW Family that I was able to work with every day. It makes such a big difference working with such an amazing group of people. You will always hold a special place in my heart. Thank you all for accepting me as one of your own and making me a part of your family. Don't ever lose that.

To my family and friends, what can I say? You already know how I feel about you, but to say it again...thank you for everything. I love y'all.

A big thank you to my editor Antonia Murphy, who took my account of my journey and turned it into a story. She did such an amazing job researching facts to add, removing the boring parts, organizing, and teaching me how to write better.

To my buddy and best friend Cowboy, who was with me for most of the adventure: without you, I would have never lived long enough to make it to Switzerland. You were always by my side and always there for me. You were probably one of the most well-travelled dogs ever. I miss you, my friend.

To our little girl Luna who was our angel, keeping us smiling through such a difficult time. We miss you tremendously, but are very happy we could save Alma, Cass, and Coconut. Together with Eva, we have a new family and the opportunity to build a new life together.

I am thankful for my amazing wife Eva, who stood by me and supported me during these difficult times. It comforts me to witness Eva's tremendous compassion. Her golden heart is so full of love, and she's still working to save more animals, despite the pain from her loss.

I am thankful to be able to share my story with you.

You can find pictures and more details
about my adventure on my website:

randy-snow.com

You can follow me on:

Facebook: *randy.snow91*   TikTok: *@snowdog91*
Instagram: *randy.snow91*   LinkedIn: *randy-snow*

DAR Foundation Rescue Organization

Website: **Direct Donation:**
www.darfoundationrescue.org   *Zeffy Donation Form*

A portion of the proceeds from
DigidogzArt (Etsy) goes to DAR Foundation